A Century of
Brazilian History Since
❧ 1865 ❧

Borzoi Books on Latin America

General Editor
LEWIS HANKE
University of California, Irvine

A Century of Brazilian History Since
1865
ISSUES and PROBLEMS

EDITED WITH AN INTRODUCTION BY

RICHARD GRAHAM
University of Utah

Alfred·A·Knopf / New York

❧ TO ❧
Jonathan, Stephen, and Andrew

Acknowledgments

I am deeply grateful to Professor Lewis Hanke for his encouragement in this venture and, indeed, for the innovative imagination reflected in this entire series. I have also profited from the advice and guidance of Professor Stanley Stein of Princeton University. The aid of Mr. Jan Flora of Cornell University is gratefully acknowledged. The task of typing the manuscript fell to Mary Menke, Anita Reed, Eleanor Parker, and Ann Graham.

I have translated Selections 2, 4, 7, 12, 13, 16, 21, and 24 myself. Titles of the selections and material in brackets are my own. With rare exceptions, footnotes have been omitted; those that appear are the original author's unless otherwise noted.

R.G.

Contents

II. THE FIRST REPUBLIC

III. BRAZIL SINCE 1930

A Century of
Brazilian History Since
⋅§ 1865 §⋅

Introduction

Brazil and its history are complex. The country lacks unity
even today. With over 85 million people spread over more
than 3 million square miles, its regional diversity is com-
pounded by poor communications. Brazil's past is similarly
disjoined and lacks unifying threads of meaning. Nor does
one find in its history those dramatic episodes, those vibrant leaders, those bloody revolutions, or those red-hot
controversies that mark the history of Spanish America.
This book, therefore, will touch on various issues and deal
with many events rather than with any single problem or
major movement. I have chosen these selections to raise
several questions but to answer none.

Believing that each generation must necessarily rewrite
its history (if it has ever been written at all), I have included materials I have found to be of special interest
to college students I have known in the last few years.
Economic development is obviously one of our immediate
concerns and, indeed, explains why some Americans are
interested in Brazil at all. Today's judgments regarding
the rule of Emperor Pedro II, the dictatorship of Getúlio
Vargas, or the actions of the present government will partly
depend on whether these regimes advanced economic
development fast enough; how fast is fast enough is still
another knotty question. The extent to which a government
is representative in spirit and possesses the institutions
through which the people can make known their will is
another issue of our time that is inevitably raised when
studying the past. Similarly, the question of nationalism—
what it has meant for Brazilians and how it is expressed

—and the meaning of the intellectual—as an expression of his time and as portent of the future—are matters of vital concern today. And, finally, the moral, value-laden questions that are implied in each one of the preceding ones must be considered, whether the subject is nineteenth-century slavery or twentieth-century foreign aid.[1]

Brazil, alone among all the Latin American countries, emerged from its colonial status without a serious military encounter. When Napoleon's forces invaded Portugal in 1807, the mad Queen Maria I, her son João the Prince Regent, and their court fled to Brazil as a government in exile. João, who later succeeded Maria as João VI, raised Brazil to the rank of kingdom in 1815 so that he could remain surrounded by its tropical charms even after the Napoleonic threat had been removed. When he was finally forced to return to Portugal by revolutionary disturbances there, he left his son in Rio; this young and impetuous Prince Regent, encouraged by his father, decided to sacrifice allegiance to Portugal in exchange for an immediate crown. He declared Brazil independent in 1822 and became its first constitutional Emperor.

After nine years, however, the Brazilian aristocracy, disturbed by his increasing tendency to surround himself with Portuguese favorites, drove him from power in 1831. He abdicated in behalf of his five-year-old son. A regency was then set up; it guided Brazil through its most turbulent days, days in which Brazil flirted with republicanism but never entirely lost its loyalty to the young monarch-to-be. In 1840 the latter assumed the crown as Pedro II. Within ten years he had, by wise appointments made with good advice, crushed the various smoldering and active rebellions that had previously swept the country, asserted his personal

---

[1] See how I have related several of the selections in the present volume to some of these questions in "Teaching Brazilian History," *The History Teacher,* II, no. 3 (March, 1969), pp. 00–00.

leadership, and launched Brazil on the road to economic
and political stability.

The next fifteen years were years of peace and progress.
The parliamentary system functioned smoothly, for Pedro
II had put together a moderate government and sheared
off extremes of right and left. Statesmen trained in local
law schools since their establishment in 1827—when Brazil made its first attempt at higher education—were now
able to provide steady leadership. Economic growth was
marked. Foreigners and Brazilians organized railroad companies and urban services. Life in the cities—especially
in Rio de Janeiro—was increasingly modeled on the European example. Coffee exports from the province of Rio
de Janeiro rapidly augmented, soon outdistancing the value
of sugar, Brazil's traditional export crop. Yet the very
progress made possible by stability gave rise to dissatisfaction.

The War of the Triple Alliance (1865–1870), or, as it
is called in Brazil, the Paraguayan War, was the sea squall
that ended these halcyon days. Its causes are still debated
(Selections 8, 9, and 10), but its effects upon the Brazilian
establishment were shattering. Nerves had been rubbed
raw by the frustrations of prosecuting the war; it was no
longer possible to find a middle way in public affairs.
The Europeanized urban classes became painfully aware
of the inadequacies of the ruling elite of landed aristocrats.
The technological backwardness of the country, the vast-
ness of the sparsely settled western areas, the outworn
slave-labor system, and the inefficiency of Brazil's bureaucracy filled through nepotism were felt especially by
the urban classes who bore the burden of financing the
war and filling the ranks of its armies. The young military
officers were disenchanted. Contact with allied republican
nations stimulated criticism of the monarchy. Slavery was
ridiculed even by the Paraguayans who consistently referred
to the Brazilians as *macacos* (monkeys). The officers

returned home anxious to revitalize their country. Brazil could no longer be the same.

In 1868 the political consensus began to give way. The dismissal of a ministry led to the reestablishment of a Liberal Party and the publication in 1869 of a manifesto demanding significant modifications of the constitution, especially the limitation of the Emperor's power. That same year the Club Radical was formed to demand even more thoroughgoing reforms. The following year many of these dissidents joined in issuing the Republican Manifesto calling for the end of the Empire for the sake of greater democracy and individual freedom. Political protest mounted to its climax in 1889 when a small group of military officers, egged on and cajoled by impatient republicans, overthrew the Empire.

But meanwhile, the economic bases of Brazilian society were also being transformed. Railroads increased from about 300 miles in 1865 to some 6,000 in 1890. Coffee spread into the new area of west-central São Paulo and pumped new wealth into the economy, bringing to the fore a new group of landed entrepreneurs. Immigrants began to arrive to work the coffee plantations. Port cities and provincial capitals burgeoned. Textile manufacturing was finally established on a sound foundation. Other industries such as iron foundries, shoe and hat factories, breweries, and tanneries multiplied; even the manufacture of paper, glass, cigars, soap, and matches achieved significant proportions. The career of Irineu Evangelista de Souza, the baron (later viscount) of Mauá, must be seen within this context. Selection 3 presents a favorable view of this entrepreneur and Selection 4 a sharply revisionist one, but neither challenges the significance of his achievements.

All these forces pushed Brazil toward an accelerating economic development which the political and social structures failed to accompany. Considerable controversy has arisen over the role in all this of the Emperor Pedro II

(Selections 1 and 2). Historians long insisted on his private virtues although today these are often considered irrelevant to any judgment regarding his governmental performance. Two more significant questions have arisen, however. First, did Pedro II exercise great power, or was he circumscribed by the Constitution and the English example so frequently cited by the statesmen of his day? And second, was the progress of Brazil under his administration little or great considering, on the one hand, the magnificent opportunity offered by the long years of political stability and, on the other, the miserably backward condition of Brazil when he took over and the alleged lack of good men upon whom he could count?

Slavery was closely related to the imperial regime. Since the landed elite that surrounded the Emperor was almost entirely made up of slave owners, the abolition of this institution in 1888 is widely recognized as one of the major factors that precipitated the end of the Empire the following year. One reason for the end of slavery was the increasing awareness that slavery was holding back Brazilian development. At the time, of course, there was much argument about this, but now it is hard to find anyone to uphold the opposite point of view, at least for the 1880s. I have, therefore, contented myself in presenting the forceful statement in this regard made by Joaquim Nabuco, one of the most prominent abolitionists (Selection 7). Beyond this point, however, there is little agreement regarding Brazilian slavery. Some believe the Emperor was chiefly responsible for ending the institution, but others insist he resisted abolition until the last moment. Some believe Parliament decreed abolition under the pressure of public opinion, but others point to the use of force to bring about this action. Most significant in its extra-Brazilian implications, however, is the controversy over the nature of the slave institution in Brazil, especially its relative harshness. The debate stretches over the entire course of its history there, and its supposed benevolence has been used to condemn the practices of other societies. Perhaps one major difficulty has been a failure to carefully differentiate various periods and regional modifications. Both selections presented here (5 and 6) deal specifically with the nineteenth century, but probably not with the same area.

The two groups who were chiefly responsible for the eventual end of the Empire—which followed the abolition of slavery by eighteen months—were the new coffee planters and the new urban interests. In the areas of São Paulo that, after 1865, were converted from subsistence crops and virgin forest into coffee plantations there arose a new group of men. With the enthusiasm of men on the way up they attacked the land, driving their insufficient slaves, borrowing money, engaging in battles over land, acquiring more, pushing westward. They looked upon their land as capital rather than as a guarantee of position. They acquired it in order to produce wealth, and if old solutions did not work, they would try new ones. These planters were landed entrepreneurs. They demonstrated their innovating spirit by adopting a new crop, using novel techniques to process it, demanding a more plentiful and flexible source of labor than could be provided by slavery, and enthusiastically welcoming the railroads, which they often built themselves. Eventually, they also invested in industry. Many of them were to be among the most vocal elements to demand political change in the late 1880s.

Increasing export trade also encouraged the rise of new urban sectors, and in the cities several groups demanded more rapid change. The military officers had not been drawn from the landed aristocracy, and during the Paraguayan War they had developed not only a consciousness of their country's backwardness but also an awareness of their common bond and a belief in their own superior honor, patriotism, and disinterestedness. They were dis-

satisfied with their peacetime status and looked to the
future with hope of a better era. They were closely related
to the civilian engineers, many of whom had begun their
training at military schools. The engineers were also in
close touch with another new-fledged group formed by
industrialists. To this urban set must be added the doctors
and lawyers who, despite their connections with the landed
aristocracy, were impelled by their contact with metropolitan society and their foreign travel to adopt the new
values of the city.

The republican movement gathered strength from the
new planters and the urban groups. The São Paulo planters
were dissatisfied with the slowness with which the imperial
government reacted to new conditions and, perhaps most
important, with the continued predominance in government
of men drawn either from the decadent northeastern sugar
areas or the declining coffee regions of the Paraíba valley.
The abolition of slavery meant an expanded money economy and an increase in consumption; the failure of the
old regime to expand the currency despite these growing
needs added to the unhappiness of both manufacturers
and planters. The continued connections between the Emperor and the older planters further alienated the urban
groups anxious for development. All that was finally needed
to topple the Empire was to mobilize the military officers
for a show of force at the right moment. This the republicans succeeded in doing, and the Emperor was deposed
without a struggle on November 15, 1889.

But the newly victorious element split into its two com-
ponent parts almost immediately. The military, by virtue
of their contribution, saw themselves as spokesmen for
the urban groups. They organized the provisional government and supplied the first two presidents. They moved
into the important government posts and many of the un-
important ones. The coffee planters, on the other hand,
defended their bases of operation by preventing the mili-

tary from taking over the government of São Paulo and built up their own state militia, biding their time. Their chance was not long in coming. The military officers fell to fighting among themselves, a major revolt broke out in southernmost Brazil, the navy sought to recover by force the prestige and position it had lost by earlier ineptitude, and the coffee planters proposed their terms: they would support the military faction then in power in exchange for the election and installation of a civilian coffee planter. The soldiers agreed, and in 1894 Prudente de Morais Barros became President.

The civilians set up a governmental system that created relative stability at the national level and allowed un-limited growth to the coffee export trade. Foreigners were much impressed. Regular elections, separation of powers, and a businesslike leadership were calculated to attract the sympathies of outsiders. Modern and extensive port works were installed in Rio de Janeiro, and the city was cleared of yellow fever and other epidemics and generally beautified. The Third Pan American Congress was held there in 1906, occasioning the first official visit abroad of the United States Secretary of State. Brazil's delegate was a prominent figure at the Hague Peace Conference (Selection 11). Brazil's diplomatic representatives were invariably urbane, well versed in international law, fluent in French and English, and white. José Honório Rodrigues, in fact, refers to them as "whitewashed" (Selection 23).

But the realities of government were quite different. The coffee planters of São Paulo and Minas Gerais, with the suitably remunerated aid of cattlemen in Rio Grande do Sul, formed a small inverted triangle of power whose apex rested upon the President of the republic. As the agent of that oligarchy, his power was immense outside the coffee areas; one author dubbed him "His Majesty the President." Working through a pyramidal structure of loyalties, he controlled the *coronéis* (landed political bosses) throughout the backlands of Brazil. The victory of the planters seemed complete.

But the urban groups could not be dismissed so easily. During the 1890s the shopkeepers and bureaucrats of the cities became almost psychotic because of the threat of proletarianization promoted by the inflationary tendencies that coffee oligarchs for a time encouraged. The result was the "jacobinism" or xenophobic nationalism of that period, often directed—as it had been during the first half of the nineteenth century—against ambitious, hardworking Portuguese immigrants. Italians had also poured into the country since the late 1880s. At first they worked the coffee lands, but increasingly they went to the cities where they even competed with their ex-employers in establishing industrial and commercial enterprises. The military officers continued to have more affinity for these middle classes in the cities than for the war lords of the interior.

The division was not always clear-cut, of course. In 1910, for instance, José Gomes Pinheiro Machado, the political boss of Rio Grande do Sul and an erstwhile friend of coffee plantation interests, successfully supported Hermes de Fonseca, the military candidate, against Rui Barbosa, a member of the urban sector, but now allied with some coffee planters. But through another prism one can see that Pinheiro Machado, perhaps unconsciously, was seeking to weld oligarchic and urban interests into a national party. The measure of his failure is to be seen in the dismal results of military efforts to destroy the power of the backland *coronéis* in Pernambuco and Bahia in 1911. Pinheiro Machado, quick to perceive the lack of success of the policies he himself had encouraged, abandoned the cause.

But some military officers continued to search for a means of destroying that oligarchic system and installing a modernizing, urban-oriented, nationalistic government. In 1922 young lieutenants loyal to Hermes da Fonseca—

who charged that the elections of that year had been fraudulently conducted—unsuccessfully revolted in Rio de Janeiro. Thus was born the movement known as *tenentismo* (Selection 14). The ideals for which the young lieutenants fought were shared by other groups. The intellectuals in the cities, especially in São Paulo, sickened by the crass materialism of the coffee planters-turned-industrialists, launched a new artistic-literary movement during the Week of Modern Art also, significantly, in 1922. Their forms were often linked to new currents in Europe, but their goal was to find their identity within their own heritage and their own culture, within their own racial mixture and their own history, within their own fields and their own rivers (Selection 15).

The role of Getúlio Vargas in giving political expression to these dreams is crucial. Although his rise has sometimes been attributed principally to urban demands for a nationalistic and developmental government, it seems more realistic to think of him as succeeding—where his fellow Rio Grandense Pinheiro Machado had failed—in uniting in one program the demands of urban and rural groups.

His success, and that of his later emulator in this respect, Juscelino Kubitschek, in satisfying both the urban "middle groups" and the rural aristocracy held Brazil together until the 1960s. Acting sometimes as dictator (1930–1934, 1937–1945) and sometimes as President (1934–1937, 1950–1954), Vargas began by buying off the coffee planters through an ambitious price-support program launched in the face of a world-wide depression and dwindling government revenues. This action amounted to pump-priming perhaps far in excess, proportionately, of anything tried elsewhere at that time. Thus the planters were happy, for the price of their coffee fell by less than one-third while the world price for Brazilian coffee plummeted by two-thirds. The urban manufacturers were happy to find an expanding market for their goods at the very time when imported items, because of a falling exchange rate, became prohibitively expensive. Their factories now began operating at full capacity, and industrial output went up 50 percent between 1929 and 1937. And urban workers were happy, for employment opportunities increased and their salaries, both real and in currency, went up. Furthermore, extensive social welfare legislation became law in Brazil, and, although vast sectors of the working population were not covered and although much of it was not applied, the workers felt more secure than ever before. That Vargas' attitude was basically paternalistic and aimed at keeping the workers satisfied so they would not upset the alliance he had constructed between industrialists and landholders was then beside the point. And his political methods were offensive to only a small liberal minority (Selections 16 and 17).

Juscelino Kubitschek managed to continue this spectacular juggling act during his administration (1955–1960). The expansion of Brazil's industrial complex was astronomical. Vargas had laid the basis with his American-financed government-owned steel plant. Others had later built privately owned mills. Overnight, Kubitschek created an automobile industry, so that today more than half of Brazilian vehicles are Brazilian-made from Brazilian steel with hardly a single imported part. The annual average real growth of the gross domestic product during the period 1955–1961 was 6.1 percent. Practically all consumer goods and nearly half the capital goods sold in Brazil by 1960 were Brazilian-made. It had been a period of unprecedented growth characterized by a developmental spirit among the young experts who surrounded the President.

But all was not well. The trick of standing on divergent and increasingly distant bases became more and more difficult. The very forces of change that had been launched were now responsible for the end of the arrangement (cf.

Selection 19). The inflationary policies that had accompanied much of this growth created special problems for the lower-middle class in the cities. These people had risen to their positions at least partly because of inflation, yet it constantly threatened them with loss of status. The rich were not so endangered for they had both the resources and the skills to cope with this; in fact, the inflationary mentality became characteristic of this group and many fortunes were multiplied many times over, even in real terms. But the great bulk of the urban residents perched precariously on their positions and were driven nearly mad with the prospect of losing them. Their plight was translated into violent outcries against officeholders (although many of them similarly profited from these offices) and strident denunciations of the planners and technocrats as agents of a foreign ideology. Development is, after all, in some ways the equivalent of subversion, for it means the destruction of the status quo.

In the countryside there were also problems. Not only had the landed class become more diversified and therefore less easily satisfied, but the position of all landowners had become more precarious as a result of the increasing demand for social justice. In 1960, 3 percent of the farms in Brazil accounted for 53 percent of the land, and the landowners were quick to perceive the danger of broadening political self-consciousness among the peasants. Not only was the population rapidly expanding because of health and sanitation programs, but better communications with the cities made the plight of those who remained on the land increasingly evident. In 1955 workers rose up on one northeastern plantation and forcibly seized the land. They were later granted legal title to it, and a movement of "Peasant Leagues" was launched to effect the same result elsewhere. Other rural workers flocked to the cities where they crowded the slums and exacerbated political tensions. Urban intellectuals who had rarely

ventured into the countryside now became inflamed at
evident injustices. And although Kubitschek's technicians
of development pointed out the need for land reform as a
prerequisite for the agricultural development that would
stem the tide of migrants, the President concentrated on
finding employment for them in industries.

Kubitschek persistently avoided thoroughgoing reforms.
But his successors were forced to face these issues. He
ignored the problem of rural labor; ignored the problem of
agricultural development, which would have meant land
reform and other changes in the status quo; ignored the
need for basic structural changes. Instead, he bought off
the urban workers by granting wage hikes; bought off the
industrialists by granting government credit; and bought
off the rural discontented by offering jobs in the construction of the expensive, though doubtless valuable, new
capital city of Brasília.

These contradictions were perhaps best expressed by
Jânio Quadros, the immediate successor of Kubitschek.
Elected with the support of coffee planters, he yet vaguely
desired land reform; in favor of Brazilian industrialists
now threatened with the overwhelming flood of American
capital attracted by Kubitschek, he yet managed to give
some the impression he was anticapitalist; nationalistically
anxious to play the cold war game to Brazil's sole benefit
(Selection 23), he was accused of being soft on communism. His problems—perhaps more the result of his
time than of his temperament—led to his resignation after
eight months.

He was succeeded constitutionally by Vice-President
João Goulart. A labor minister under Vargas and a tool
of the ex-President in his effort to marshal the support of
the unions, Goulart was distrusted by the military and
feared by conservatives (Selection 20). Installed only at
the price of giving up his power under a hastily established
parliamentary system, he was finally recognized as "real"

President in January 1963, after a national plebiscite. Goulart was completely unable to continue the policies of welding together such disparate elements as landed oligarchs and urban workers; he discredited every cause he took up. Economic growth slowed drastically while prices soared more wildly than ever. His inexperienced efforts to slow inflation required sacrifices from laborers that they were obstinately unwilling to make; his effort to compensate the left by instituting land reform met with the unalterable opposition of the right. His attempts to declare a state of siege were hampered by his naïve willingness to submit his proposal to Congress according to constitutional forms: not only did he not get the authorization, but he tipped off his opponents as to his increasing desperation. Finally returning to the arms of labor, he became stridently radical during the last months of his regime. Hoping to build upon the force of enlisted men and noncommissioned officers as Vargas before him had built upon lieutenants, he provided the officers with the excuse they had been awaiting. He was overthrown by a military coup on the night of March 31, 1964. Despite the much vaunted tradition of stability in Brazil, the officers found many earlier examples to follow (Selection 22).

The new regime—led by Officer–Presidents elected by a purged Congress—has had to face many problems. But the principal one is in a sense political: Can the same policies continue to satisfy rural oligarchs, progressive planters, industrialists, rural and urban workers, and the middle classes of the cities? If not, which interests will be sacrificed? Before another century has passed we will know the answer. But by then students will be asking other questions.

I

The Empire

Anfriso Fialho

The Emperor Pedro II: A Favorable View

No one figure is more central to the nineteenth-century history of Brazil than Pedro II. A man of quiet, indeed placid, temperament, he nevertheless became the subject of much controversy during his time, a controversy that has not yet subsided. Some observers then and now have emphasized his moral virtues, marital fidelity, and love of learning; but others have insisted that the essential question is whether he advanced his country's progress. Even here there is no agreement: some point to political stability as an achievement, but others consider it a sign of stagnation; some say he fostered growth in the face of hidebound conservatism, but others demonstrate the sorry state of Brazil at the time of his overthrow; some argue that his adherence to constitutionalism prevented more effective action, but others insist on the great power he wielded and ask why it was directed toward preserving the old instead of creating the new.

From Anfriso Fialho, "Biographical Sketch of Dom Pedro II, Emperor of Brazil," trans. M. A. Henry, in Smithsonian Institution, *Annual Report of the Board of Regents* (Washington, 1877), pp. 173, 176–178, 182, 189–195, 198–203.

*Rarely is it possible to find such contrasting opin-
ions expressed by the same man as is the case in this
and the subsequent selection. European-educated Anfriso Fialho was a member of the growing number of
unemployed elite in imperial Brazil. Born in 1840, he
went to secondary school in Germany, fought in the
Brazilian army during the Paraguayan War, and later
entered law school in Portugal. He then moved to
Brussels, where he finished his legal training at the
age of thirty-three. He was still in Europe when he
published a short book entitled* Don Pedro II, em-
pereur du Brésil: notice biographique (*Brussels,
1876*). The following selection is taken from an
English translation made at that time with a charac-
teristically nineteenth-century phraseology.*

About a year ago the telegraph announced the intention
of the Emperor of Brazil to visit the United States and
the countries of the north of Europe he had omitted in
his first tour in 1871. Remembering the favorable manner
in which the journals had at that time spoken of the distinguished traveler and of his reign, which has lasted now
for forty-five years, I determined to prepare an account
of both for the public, although under a very abridged
form. . . .

Dom Pedro II . . . was born at Rio de Janeiro on the
2d of December, 1825; and had hardly completed his fifth
year when his august father abdicated in his favor, in accordance with the constitution. . . . [Pedro II] very naturally determined to make a man of himself, to seriously
prepare not only to guard against danger, but also to meet
it if necessary. A happy inspiration taught him that the
surest way to this end was the acquirement of superior
knowledge of science in all its branches. The most learned
professors, national and foreign, to be found in the coun-

try or that could be obtained from abroad had been provided for his classical studies, and later, others were entrusted with his instruction in philosophy and mathematics as well as the natural, moral, and political sciences. Although pursuing all these branches with equal facility and like ardor, he had for the natural sciences a marked preference amounting to enthusiasm. . . .

From this period [the defeat of Rosas in 1852], really began that progress which excites the admiration of all who compare the Brazil of the present with the Brazil of twenty-five years ago. This beautiful era in the history of the vast empire commenced with the abolition of the slave trade—an immense step toward civilization—followed by a veritable enthusiasm for commercial and industrial enterprises: then were laid the first railroads, the especial lines of which, such as those of the State, received the guarantee of an interest of 7 percent; the companies for river and maritime navigation were largely increased; Europe was brought into communication with Brazil by means of steam; gas was introduced into all the great cities, and good roads were opened. Most of these enterprises gave to agricultural industry, especially to the culture of coffee, sugar, tobacco, and cotton, a marked impulse, and were thus of material benefit to all classes of society. . . .

[During the war with Paraguay] another circumstance also proved both how much Dom Pedro had at heart the reparation of the affront to his country, and the entire confidence he had in final victory: after the reverse of Curupaití he had confided the chief command of the Brazilian troops to the head of the Conservative Party, Marshal Caxias, a measure which was approved by the Liberal ministry under Senator Zacarias. Some time after, the reciprocal confidence between the general and this body was disturbed to such a degree that both offered to resign. . . . Dom Pedro was now obliged to choose be-

tween a new Liberal ministry, which could inspire the
confidence neither of the general-in-chief nor yet of those
who were opposed to him, and a Conservative ministry
which would be willing to afford the marshal every possible means to secure the victory. These considerations decided the Emperor in favor of the latter, which was pre-
sided over by the Viscount de Itaboraí, who was obliged to
dissolve the Chamber of Deputies for refusing to support
him (July, 1868). . . .

The war did not prevent the imperial government from
taking all the administrative measures the circumstances
would allow to increase the prosperity of the country. The
navigation of the Amazon was opened to foreign nations;
new lines of railroad were projected, and the construction
of those which had been commenced was not allowed to
be interrupted; in a word, progress continued with a firm
and assured pace, and, except a slight increase in customs
duties and of land and personal taxes, absolutely nothing
indicated that the nation was engaged in a formidable contest. Commercial transactions received such an impulse
that large fortunes were made as if by enchantment. . . .

Peace concluded, the government, far from resting upon
its laurels, employed every means to draw from the experience gained during the war knowledge that would be
useful in the future and render the country better able to
meet with promptitude attacks from its turbulent neighbors or other nations. The leaders who had most distinguished themselves upon land and sea during the war
were consulted as to the best measures for this end; and,
in accordance with the information received from them,
new iron-clad vessels were ordered, among which should
be mentioned the frigate *Independência,* still in course of
construction at London and one of the largest in the
world; the army was re-organized; the mode of recruiting
by force, hitherto employed, was replaced by the system
of conscription; corporal punishment, so derogatory to

human dignity, was abolished, and the pay of the officers was increased a third. . . .

Dom Pedro had for a long time wished to visit Europe, but the accomplishment of his desire had been postponed, at one time by troubles at home, at another by differences with foreign nations. . . . Dom Pedro asked and obtained leave of absence for a year, and started for Europe in the month of May, 1871, under the name of Dom Pedro d'Alcantara, confiding the regency of the empire to his daughter, the Countess d'Eu. . . . The first stopping place of the imperial tourists was Lisbon. Upon the arrival of the Emperor, Louis I, his nephew, came to meet him and offered to suspend the rules of quarantine and conduct him immediately to his palace. Dom Pedro, firmly determined to travel as a private gentleman, not only refused to accept this offer but also to pass the four days of quarantine in a man-of-war the King placed at his disposal. He lodged, therefore, in the common lazaretto with all the passengers who had landed at Lisbon. He passed several days in the beautiful capital, and then went by rail to Spain. . . . After Spain he visited France, England, Belgium, Germany, Switzerland, Austria, Italy, and Egypt. He took advantage of his journey to lay the foundations of several treaties of commerce and friendship, but particularly of extradition, which were afterwards consummated.

In these different countries, of which he knew as much as could be learned from written descriptions, Dom Pedro made a careful examination of the works of art, of science, and of industry, the schools, universities, and scientific societies, whose meetings he delighted to attend. He invited to his table distinguished men of all classes, and surprised more than one Diogenes in his tub. Everywhere and to everybody he exhibited much more knowledge than is generally possessed by the heads of nations and, on his return to Brazil, honored with the most distinguished decorations the men of letters, arts, and science with whom he had been in relation. In certain charitable institutions and in the poor quarter of several large cities he left substantial souvenirs of his visit. Dom Pedro was decorated on this journey with the Order of the Garter and also received diplomas from several learned societies, among which we may mention that of member of the natural history section of the French Institute, a deserved reward for his profound study of this branch of knowledge. In short, the journey was a success and of great importance to Brazil, as the Emperor was enabled to refute the errors that superficial or malevolent writers had spread all over Europe in regard to the country. . . .

The return of Dom Pedro to Brazil gave the people another opportunity of showing their attachment by an enthusiastic welcome and a brilliant reception at the capital. One of his first acts was to abolish the *baise main,* a custom which had been inherited from the ancient kings of Portugal.

Then he hastened to introduce every useful art and custom he had seen abroad compatible with the climate, institutions, and national habits of the country. . . . Brazil was then united by the telegraph with Europe, the United States, and the republics of La Plata. Several other works of public interest, such as the construction of new railways and the opening of new roads, &c., were undertaken or received new impulse from the government. . . .

In political and intellectual affairs there was radical reform, especially in the reorganization of primary schools, of higher schools, and the revision of the electoral law. The solicitude Dom Pedro had always felt in regard to public instruction proves conclusively how entirely he was convinced that it is the condition *sine qua non* of all real and lasting progress. It is, therefore, not surprising that during his journey his attention should have been especially directed to this branch of public administration. After adopting the methods and programs of study which

seemed to him the best, he caused a number of really palatial buildings to be erected with spacious gardens attached,
to be used as public schools for children of both sexes; and
in order to render study agreeable, the luxury and provisions for comfort in these establishments were so great
as to be condemned as extravagance by those opposed to
the projects of the Emperor. In the high schools, reform was
introduced in the regulation of examinations. These were
rendered so much more difficult as to excite the manifest
hostility of the students; but the increased rigor was really
necessary, as the diplomas conferred by the scientific cor-
porations had ceased to be regarded with much confidence.
The central school was reorganized and converted into a
polytechnic institution, similar to the Belgian schools for
engineers. Lastly, a school of mines was formed in the province of Minas, the richest in precious minerals; and now it
is proposed to found at Rio a university, with due consideration, however, for the faculties of law and medicine existing
in the provinces.

The reform of the electoral law is one of the greatest
benefits Brazil has received from the very hand, so to say,
of the present Emperor. The old law was full of flaws which
might allow a party in power to remain so continually, were
it not for the prerogatives accorded the Emperor by the constitution. No party at the head of the administration had
desired to reform this law precisely because of the advantage to be drawn from its defects, but, once in the opposition, there was no want of condemnation of the frauds
and violence committed by the agents and friends of the
government during the elections. The greatest inconven-
iences resulting from this defective law were, on the one
hand, the impossibility of knowing whether the parliamentary majority represented really the opinion of the people,
and, on the other, the want of any security that the minority would be represented. Also, every dissolution of the
houses of parliament was followed by a unanimous cham-

ber, evidently the creation of the ministry; and, even if it had not such general support, it could always exercise great influence upon legislative decisions because of its power over a large number of public functionaries; that is to say, on account of the number of public offices at its disposal.

For the purpose not only of putting an end to the complaints of parties not in power, but also and principally to govern in accordance with the real desires of the nation—the first duty of every honest government—Dom Pedro determined to reform the electoral law, and on the occasion of the opening of parliament in 1874, entered into a formal engagement to prevent, in the future, electoral abuses.

The Liberal Party desired election by one degree, that is, direct election; but the constitution positively required election by two degrees, that is, indirect. This was an insurmountable obstacle to the Emperor, for he knew that too frequent alteration of the organic laws of a country ends in political disorganization. He therefore confined his attention to such changes in the old system as would render parliament more independent of the government. Among the improvements of the new law was the decree that the holding of the office of representative was incompatible with the tenure of any other charge remunerated by the state, and that the government could not nominate any deputy or senator to an office six months before or after the elections. Should this loyal attempt at reform by the Emperor be unsuccessful, we are convinced he would propose to the people to change the constitution, rather than have the national vote continually misconstrued. . . .

Dom Pedro's activity is extraordinary. He rises at 6 o'clock, reads certain news journals while his secretary looks over others and marks passages worthy of consideration, attends to business until half past 9, breakfasts rapidly, then gives audience to the public; after which he generally visits the schools, arsenals, fortresses, or attends a session of a scientific society, &c. He dines at 5, again gives audience to the people, and then resumes business, if he does not go to the theater (of which he is very fond), to a concert, a ball, or some private entertainment. He never retires before midnight.

When visiting the establishments of instruction, whether private or belonging to the state, in the capital or in the provinces, he assists in the examination of the pupils and in the distribution of prizes, and makes note on these occasions of the name, family, and place of birth of those who distinguish themselves in their studies. More than one thus noticed has afterward found in the Emperor a powerful protector.

Dom Pedro not only encourages letters and the arts, he also renders important aid to industrial societies of general utility, either from his own purse by the purchase of shares, or by demanding subsidy for them from the legislative bodies.

He presides twice a week at the Council of State. The session commences at 9 o'clock in the evening, and lasts sometimes until 1 in the morning. Each minister gives an account in his presence of all the matters in his department requiring the imperial signature; the Emperor listens with attention, and occasionally asks for some explanation. If the matter is of importance—especially if it touches the rights or the purses of the citizens—he will not allow a decision on the same day, but takes time to study the subject carefully, giving his opinion at the next session. If it is a radical innovation he employs a longer time in examining all its details, consults the Council of State, and adopts it at last only if convinced that it is really and intelligently desired, and will be of profit to the people; for his long experience in the government of men has taught him that reform must be carefully considered, must be opportune and very evidently beneficial before it is adopted, in order that progress may be made. In this respect he is a liberal conservative, as every head of a nation should be who desires to respect the laws and at the same time advance civilization.

One would suppose from this active interference of the Emperor in the affairs of state, that the ministry exercises but little power. But this is not the case, for the Emperor has for the constitution, and for the public offices it creates, an almost religious respect. It is sufficient to say that he has not once during his long reign made use of the veto power given him by the constitution. He has never forced his own wishes upon any of his ministers; he leaves them entire freedom of action. But this very respect for the laws of the nation, as well as his own experience, has taught him the necessity of exercising his sovereign attributes, which he does, taking counsel only of his own conscience.

This loyal conduct, this benevolent interference on the part of the sovereign in the affairs of the country, has nevertheless been attacked as unconstitutional, as too personal a government. Those who pretend that the control of a nation should be left exclusively to the ministers and parliamentary majorities, rest upon the celebrated maxim: *"The constitutional king reigns, but does not govern."* This is not the place to discuss this important question, but as to the maxim we cannot refrain from declaring, with Guizot, that it has no solid foundation. . . . The maxim, moreover, is not in accordance with the Brazilian constitution which confers upon the sovereign not only control over the political powers governing the nation but also especial attributes to be exercised by him exclusively. The accusation therefore that the Emperor is illegal in his personal government is without foundation.

We have seen that Dom Pedro gives audience to the public twice a day. On these occasions he exhibits the qualities of a truly liberal sovereign, and shows that he cares as much for the interests of his Brazilian family as for his own. In fact, he receives everyone—foreigners or his own people—with affability and kindness, pressing the hand of those he regards especially. If an artist or a savant presents himself, Dom Pedro does not allow him to depart without some conversation upon his especial pursuit; if one of his acquaintances, he inquires with interest for the health of the different members of his family and interchanges with him some familiar and pleasant remarks. To claimants he has become somewhat reserved in manner on account of the great number who have imposed upon his kindness, and also because he does not wish to encroach upon the attributes of his ministers. Still, he listens with patience and attention; making from time to time an objection, or giving counsel; but he does not trouble the ministers with their pretensions, unless justice, equity, or benevolence require. If a complaint is made to him either from subaltern officials, who are very apt to suppose injustice has been done when they have not been promoted fast enough to suit their supposed deserts, or from a disappointed office-seeker, or from anyone whatever, Dom Pedro takes the trouble to inquire into and discuss the cause of his discontent. He endeavors to reconcile as much as possible the duties his political position impose upon him with his own inclinations which always lead him to clemency and benevolence. Thus every year, on the occasion of certain religious, national and dynastic festivals, he pardons the condemned and the criminals. . . .

As to the liberality of the Brazilian monarch, it is manifested in various ways: sometimes by general almsgiving (he causes several hundreds of centimes to be distributed to the poor every Saturday), sometimes by especial donations, either voluntary or by request, sometimes in annual pensions to certain meritorious persons, and frequently in sums of money given for the education of promising youth, often large enough to allow them to prosecute their studies in Europe. It is an edifying proof of his religious feelings and of his Christian humility, that every year on holy Friday he washes publicly the feet of the poor in the imperial chapel, and that during the procession of the *Corpus Christi* he assists in carrying the dais throughout the ceremony.

The qualities we have noticed are sufficiently indicative of what Dom Pedro is in private; it is hardly necessary to say that he is an excellent husband and model father. The Empress, his faithful companion since 1843, is an admirable woman, a providence to the poor and the orphan; to know her many virtues and not love her is impossible. The heiress presumptive to the throne, the only child left him, has received a careful education befitting her rank and the office she will assume in the empire. Her political instruction, promoted by several European tours, especially in England where she seemed to seek in Queen Victoria an example for future imitation, is the exclusive charge of her august father. Her first essay in the art of government, four years ago, gave great satisfaction and promised well for the future. As she is now again in charge of the empire, Dom Pedro can travel without care, as he knows the love of the Brazilian people for their future Empress is as great and as sincere as that for their present Emperor.

When we look back over the reign of Dom Pedro, and compare the Brazil of 1831, the time of the ascension to the throne by the present Emperor—when the national wealth was, so to say, insignificant, when the existence even of society was menaced by anarchy, when there were almost no means of communication with the interior—with the Brazil of today, taking into consideration its commerce and agricultural prosperity; its numerous coast and river steamboats, its railroads and telegraph lines passing through regions of country then occupied by virginal forests; its educational institutions of every degree; and its powerful means of defense—when we remember that these two periods are separated only by an interval of forty years and reflect upon the immense progress which has been made in this comparatively short space of time, represented by the words "riches," "tranquillity," "respect," "happiness" —we have cause to be astonished and to ask if all this is the work of a single man.

It is true these great things have not been accomplished exclusively by the present Emperor of Brazil; but, as permanent head of the government, the credit for them, of right, for the most part belongs to him. It is at his instigation that important measures of the administration have been undertaken; it is he who has the right to approve or reject the projects of reform; it is he, in short, who has selected the men who have aided him in the realization of his philosophical ideal of prosperity for his people. The Brazilians render him full justice and thank him for the position their country occupies among civilized nations.

◄§2§►

Anfriso Fialho

The Emperor Pedro II:
A Critical View

Embittered by his failure to secure support for his schemes to create central sugar factories and disillusioned by the limited possibilities for advancement open to him despite what he considered his excellent education, Anfriso Fialho became a virulent republican. The virtues of the Emperor that he had earlier extolled now became his vices. Excited to a fever pitch by the defeat of a Liberal ministry in 1885, Fialho published a pamphlet that admitted the unlikelihood of revolution and called for a new constitutional convention.

His principal complaint against Pedro II was that he had failed to foster the country's progress. To make this charge stick he first had to convince the reader that Pedro II had the power to promote or retard it. Although strident and often irrational, he here sums up the principal points of those who then and since have critically examined the Emperor.

Translated from Anfriso Fialho, *Processo da monarchia brazileira: necessidade da convocação de uma constituinte* (Rio de Janeiro: Typographia da Gazeta de Noticias, 1885), pp. 5–27.

I

In 1876 when the Emperor began his second trip to Europe and I was residing in Brussels as military attaché to the Brazilian legation, I resolved to take advantage of this opportunity to make our country better known in the civilized Old World. . . . Since I had, until that time, passed the greater part of my life either in Europe, where I was educated, or in a military academy in Brazil, or in the countries that were theaters for the Uruguayan and Paraguayan campaigns (1864–1870), in which I took part, I wrote a biography of the Brazilian monarch, in which I repeated the good things that I had heard about him or read in a few biographical sketches to which I had access at the time. My publication provoked on the part of some of my countrymen—both acquaintances and others—comments that greatly surprised me. Some anonymous ones sent me letters that quite frankly qualified my historical essay as servile flattery, scheming adulation, and so on; my acquaintances, however, who well knew that I am incapable of nourishing such mean sentiments, limited their criticism to warning me that I had been misled and that I did not really know the Emperor.

Thus warned, I took it upon myself to seek the truth for myself through the only trustworthy source, that is, in the facts. . . . During the investigations that I began in Europe in 1877 and continued in Brazil during the seven years since 1878, I studied, analyzed, and meditated upon the principal political and nonpolitical facts in which the Emperor played an indirect or direct role; I compared the facts of this eight-year period with those that make up our political history since he was declared of age. Furthermore, in order to interpret it better, I re-read, paying particular attention to the Roman emperors, the history of the world. I also steeped myself carefully in the revelations of Machiavelli and in the advice that he gives to heads of state in his immortal work *The Prince*.

Now, the result of this conscientious and practical study was greatly saddening. The Emperor then appeared to be so nearly the opposite of that which I had supposed he was and had said he was that it was difficult for even me to admit the results of my own research as I continued to study and know him better. . . .

The biography of the Emperor that I wrote in Brussels is the photograph of one of his faces, the one that he presents in public and on which he wears a mask of patriotism and honesty; his true story, of which this [pamphlet] is a sketch, will be the reproduction of his other face, one that is seen only by his heir presumptive —to whom he certainly must have already taught the "profession of king"—and by those . . . who have studied him carefully and with the right instruments.

Now let us look at the Emperor's plan, the existence of which I was far from suspecting in 1876. Dom Pedro II recognized—by himself or because he was taught by the monks who educated him—that the Brazilian monarchy was the only tree of its species that was cultivated in the vast soil of America and that the natural tendencies of the Brazilian people were identical with those of their American brethren, that is to say, completely republican. . . . Therefore, he very naturally resolved to oppose those tendencies by policies that had as their goal the consolidation of his monarchy or his throne. . . .

The principal ideas of the Emperor's political plan were two: (1) to become the only power in the nation so that everything and everyone, institutions and men, would depend on him and so that he might force them or steer them toward the interests of the throne, and (2) to reduce the nation to a corpse, by impeding progress and prosperity, which are its source of strength and independence. . . . In order to accomplish this plan, the

Emperor, guided by the maxims and principles taught by
Machiavelli and other authors, organized a truly ingenious
but diabolical system of government. He then put it into
practice with an ability and perseverance that clearly
demonstrate the immense ambition that drove him on. . . .

II

As to the existence of the personal power [that is, the
abuse of the moderative power ascribed to the Emperor
by the constitution], which is the heart of the imperial
plan, it is proven by the only irrefutable method by which
it can be proven, that is, by the testimony of the most
credible of the ex-ministers.

To wit, Senator Eusébio de Queiroz [Lima], ex-minister
and chief of the Conservative Party, used to say that "a
man of dignity could not be twice a minister for Dom
Pedro II," thus alluding to the fact that the monarch did
not allow a minister to govern freely. And he no longer
wished to be minister during this reign.

Senator [Antônio Francisco] Paula Sousa, ex-minister
and chief of the Liberal Party, said, referring to the
Emperor: "There's something rotten up there."

Sr. Paulino [José Soares] de Sousa, ex-minister and still
today one of the Conservative leaders, exclaimed in 1871
in the Chamber of Deputies: "Gentlemen, two centuries
ago Father Antônio Vieira said a profound truth, and it is
that in this country there is only one will" (that of the
Emperor). . . .

Now, Sr. [José Antônio] Saraiva [head of the cabinet
when this was being written] has said . . . "This business
of personal power is a false rumor because there is no
such thing with ministers who have the courage of their
convictions." To refute this allegation I shall mention only
two facts: . . .

The first of these concerns Honório Hermeto Carneiro

Leão (later the Marquis of Paraná), who was the most energetic Brazilian politician and who, therefore, can be considered a minister who most certainly had the courage of his convictions. Well, when Sr. Honório was head of the ministry in 1843 he wanted to fire one of his employees. . . . But he was unable to do so because of the implacable resistance of the Emperor. But the minister had enough dignity and courage to follow his convictions and say to the monarch: "Sir, either the customs inspector is fired or I shall resign as Your Majesty's minister." I need not remind Sr. Saraiva what was the result of this alternative that the proud and worthy minister put before the Emperor: it was the minister who was fired! The personal power, or, better, dictatorial power, the "absolutism" of the monarch won out in spite of the courageous convictions of the minister! . . .

The second historical incident took place . . . with another minister known as one of the most independent men in Brazil because of his character, his knowledge, and his means. I am speaking of Zacarias de Góes e Vasconcelos, Liberal Party chief. When he was president of the Council of Ministers in 1868, the Emperor, wanting to dismiss him in order to place the Conservatives in power, chose Salles Torres Homem as senator, he being the only adversary of the ministry in the list of nominees, the other two being members of the government party. Pedro II foresaw perfectly well what would happen. Zacarias said to the Emperor that the choice was "injudicious." The Emperor remained firm in his opinion and this president of the Council who had the courage of his convictions—as did Paraná—offered to the Emperor the same alternative as had the latter minister in 1843. Sr. Saraiva knows that once again the wish of the Emperor prevailed and that Zacarias had to resign. Of what use to the minister was the courage of his convictions? . . .

There are, however, those who affirm (some through conviction and others only to defend the Emperor) that it is the political parties that are responsible for the existence of the personal power. To them I would say that the parties are represented by their leaders; and what was the influence that individuals such as Paraná, the leader of the Conservative Party, and Zacarias, the leader of the Liberal Party, exerted over the Emperor? The facts that I cited regarding these two great party leaders prove beyond the shadow of a doubt that they could not possibly do anything more than they did in face of the caprice of an Emperor who would not abide by legality. They resigned because they did not want to surrender, nobly preferring to sacrifice themselves. . . . They resigned, I repeat, and it was the only way they had of resisting the personal power.

But the Emperor did not pay attention to this resistance, as he will not pay any attention to any other of similar nature that might be brought against him, because he knows that there is no lack of persons who want to be minister, even under the express condition of bringing oneself to say publicly that Dom Pedro is the model constitutional monarch. . . .

In a country of poor people such as Brazil, he corrupts the few who have definite means of subsistence and who have acquired a certain independence by giving them titles and so-called honors. For all the others, no matter how elevated the position he has given them, he treats them with contempt. . . . The ministers are his most docile instruments. If the minister is only a deputy, he is as pliable as one can imagine because he has a long road to travel: he wants the protection of the ministry that comes next—that is, of the new imperial instrument—in order to be reelected; he wants to be senator, counselor of state, minister once again, or at least obtain a simple employment in order to continue living. If the minister is already a senator he wants to be counselor of state, president of the cabinet, etc. And so it goes. All politicians depend on him and want to be on good terms with him. He knows this and therefore continues using them as he sees fit. . . .

Another objection [to my argument] is similar to the first: according to this view the responsibility for the personal power lies with the people. If those who accuse the people mean that they should rebel or carry out a revolution they will see later on the impossibility of such a move. In any other circumstance I would say that if the organized political parties, which are a real force capable of direction, have not been able to kill the *monster,* how could the people do so when they are scattered over a vast expanse of land and are without a plan or a leader? Tell us *how* the people could do away with the personal power! . . .

III

As to the second part of the imperial plan—reducing the nation to the state of a corpse—it is palpable for whoever cares to feel and visible for whoever cares to see. Do not be deceived by the appearances of Rio de Janeiro, which in its commerce is more foreign than Brazilian and seems an oasis in an immense desert despite the great misery that the intelligent observer can readily discover even in it. Thus the agricultural interests, the first and almost only source of the country's income, are deeply in debt; . . . there is a constant governmental deficit, which is increasing by leaps and bounds; some of the provinces cannot pay the public employees; paper money, the only currency in circulation, has depreciated about 50 percent; a few years ago, in order not to delay in satisfying our public creditors in Europe, we sold our dreadnaught, the *Independência*; presently, on days designated for payment of interest on the bonds of the public internal debt, the comptroller covers up for the lack of money saying that "the books are not yet up to date"; the state seeks part of the resources that it needs for its expenses from the lottery, that is, in the money of the poor and in gambling; beggars are organized throughout the Empire, with regular hours and definite days; . . . lawyers, doctors, and engineers are waiting for public employment in order to live, and so long as they fail to obtain it they live miserably, usually from loans that are alms in disguise; large-scale public and private prostitution is another form of begging to which a part of the population is reduced.

Poverty and *backwardness* are thus the sorry state of Brazil, as was recently confessed in Parliament by the government itself, that is by Sr. Saraiva. . . . For when a Republican deputy in the Chamber attributed to the monarchy the sad situation in which Brazil finds herself, the head of the ministry responded that "it was not the monarchy that was the cause of *our misfortune and of our backwardness*," a defense that implies a confession that the country is *backward* and *suffering.* . . .

The revenue of the Empire is equivalent to that of the city of Paris! This is the result of nearly half a century of Dom Pedro's absolutism. And how could it be otherwise if the Emperor never did what he should have done to promote national progress? How could Brazil have progressed and developed its natural resources without highways, labor, capital, public instruction, and civic and professional education, that is, without a single one of the factors that are recognized by economists as being indispensable for social progress and enrichment? And on top of all this, he has preserved slavery, which is the most powerful obstacle to progress! It would indeed have been a miracle if we had prospered and become a rich, advanced, strong, and admirable people without employing a single one of those means to this end that are recommended by political economy and especially without eradicating from our bosom the cancer of slavery.

In fact, the government of the Emperor not only never ordered the construction of highways—the first of all conditions for prosperity in a country that lives almost exclusively from agriculture—he never seriously attempted to resolve the problems of immigration and settlement, the solution of which would have brought us a great fund of intelligence, improvements, and industriousness. He never organized a plan of professional instruction or of national education. He did, however, conserve as long as he could the most destructive element of our backwardness, poverty, and moral putrefaction, that is, SLAVERY, making of this criminal institution the most active collaborator in his work of destruction in the interior. In the same way, he used yellow fever—through his Speeches from the Throne—as his principal means of propaganda against immigration.

These are the reasons why we have not prospered. The fault lies entirely with the monarchy. It is due to government by an Emperor who has done absolutely nothing of what he should have done to promote the well-being, progress, and happiness of the nation. And, as it is exclusively the Emperor who has governed the country, it follows that he is the *only* guilty one.

In the means employed to cover up his own guilt the Emperor has revealed the greatest ability in the art of deception. Faithful to his tactics of not having any certain norm of conduct in order not to give the observer the thread that could allow him to discover his secret designs, the Emperor imitates the *capoeira* [ritualized struggle]: he advances, retreats, stops, jumps to the right and to the left; he feigns the opposite of what he wants to do. . . . He errs intentionally, pretending to try; he does with one hand what he undoes with the other; . . . he employs, as Machiavelli advises, a net of deceptions, and only when all this does not work does he resort to force and the sword, but even then *in disguise*. . . .

It is thus that, on the topic of immigration and colonization, for example, his government has made great expenditures for the introduction of colonists at so much per head;
he founded a government bureau to which he gave the
pompous name of General Inspectorship of Lands and
Colonization; he bought a huge shelter for the newly arrived colonists and made a lot of noise and showed much
ostentation regarding the purchase in order to attract the
attention of the country; and he has entertained an enormous correspondence on the subject. All this while alternately taking the most appropriate measures to impede the
solution of the problem.

In like manner, in order to respond to the eventual accusation of not having constructed highways, which are
our most urgently needed means of communication, he ordered the construction of more railroads than we now need
(and even these without an intelligent plan), whose rates
are so high as to make them almost useless. . . .

Similarly, in order to make people believe that progress
—which is identified in the popular mind with the electric
telegraph—was taking place, he had a telegraphic net-
work constructed, which covered the entire Empire; but
basically his goal was to complete administrative centralization by linking all the authorities and imperial agents
spread over the length and breadth of the country to the
seat of his central government by using this perfect instrument.

Likewise, if yellow fever drives away the foreigner, he
orders the creation of a board of hygiene but pays its members miserably and does not give them sufficient prerogatives to accomplish the goal for which it was created. And
then he tops it all off by saying nearly every year in his
Speech from the Throne (the contents of which is, aside
from ministerial changes, the *only* news that is reported in
Europe) that "yellow fever," or a similar epidemic has
"broken out" or "continues to scourge the country." He

does this in order to impede the coming of immigrants to Brazil.

While he leaves the provinces almost without schools and gives a ridiculously low salary to public teachers, . . . which obliges them to resign, . . . he constructs palaces in the capital that knock your eyes out. And, to attract attention to the source of these establishments, he orders the following words engraved on the façade: *From the Government to the People.* . . .

Add to these examples the infinite number of means that the Emperor has for corrupting or deceiving his subjects—among which are the daily visits that he makes to schools, forts, barracks, and other public establishments, pretending to be interested in their prosperity and in the public welfare—and . . . one has an idea of the force of the Brazilian monarch in the art of deception. The reader will see that the secret purpose of the Emperor's visits to the schools and presence at the exams of the youngsters is to discover which are the talented youths in order that he might later "clip their wings or tie a lead weight to them." I was a resident student for four years at the Praia Vermelha Military School, to which the Emperor was a frequent visitor, and I can affirm not only that no benefit came to the school as a result of these visits but that the Emperor never proposed or suggested a single new measure or improvement.

If we now raise our eyes to the external life of the nation, what do we see? We see there also our weakness and lack of prestige. Even our victory over Paraguay is a proof of this weakness because of the immense amount of time and enormous resources that we had to expend in order to defeat, in the company of two allies (one of which is judged capable of measuring its forces with our own), a tiny, unknown, and backward republic.

This humiliating and sorry state of Brazil . . . is, of course, the result of a coldly conceived and inexorably executed plan. For Dom Pedro is convinced, as I have already said, that the wealth and individual independence of each Brazilian would be followed by the true political independence of the nation, that is, by the advent of the republic and his fall from the throne. . . .

In short, Brazil is an immense *fazenda* [plantation] that has been exploited for nearly 400 years by the Braganza dynasty. Today this *fazenda* belongs to Dom Pedro II, who, in order more securely to maintain this beautiful and profitable property, consents to its administration—but under certain conditions and under the closest supervision —by managers who are the leaders of the political parties. So one may say that Brazil is exploited by an oligarchy composed of the imperial family and the families of the political bosses. . . .

J. F. Normano

---◆➤◆◀---

Viscount Mauá
as Seen by an Admirer

*The Horatio Alger type has always attracted ad-
miration. Irineu Evangelista de Souza, baron and
later viscount of Mauá (1813–1889), was such a
man. His life spanned the period of the Empire in
Brazil, and economic historians of this era have frequently focused their attention on his work. Today,
at a time when the industrialization of Brazil has become the country's goal, he is seen as a national hero.
J. F. Normano, a European scholar who was a pioneer in Brazilian economic history, has based the
following study largely on the biography written in
1926 by the corporation lawyer Alberto de Faria.*

Peculiar was the life of this great entrepreneur. He was
a self-made man in the American sense of the word. He
started in as an apprentice, and became the greatest banker
of the southern continent, a statesman and diplomat, for
a time the financial ruler of the Atlantic coast of South
America, an associate of the Rothschilds in London, owner

From J. F. Normano, *Brazil, a Study of Economic Types* (Chapel
Hill: University of North Carolina Press, 1935), pp. 90–94.

of banks in England, the United States of America, Brazil, Uruguay and Argentina—the true international and Inter-American banker.

We can hardly imagine, now, the influence and role of Mauá in the third quarter of the nineteenth century. Beloved and hated at the time of his activity, he became neglected after his death. Monuments to Mauá are erected in many Brazilian cities; streets and places are commemorated to him; but despite all this, only recent times have brought a revival of interest in this outstanding figure and attempts are now being made to locate his real place in Brazilian history.

Mauá's activity was diversified and universal in Brazil. He introduced the steamship on the Amazon and opened up the river to the world; he adjusted Rio Grande do Sul to transatlantic communication; he created ports, was the first and greatest builder of railroads in Brazil (even without subsidy), of highways and telegraph lines; he initiated gaslight in Rio de Janeiro and other cities, was the contractor of the Canal do Mangue, the founder of textile factories, the financier of gold mines, the guiding spirit behind the laying of the submarine cable, and the most powerful individual influence in the foundation of the famous Companhia Pastoril, Agricola e Industrial with latifundia in Uruguay and Argentina. Mauá transformed Rio de Janeiro. . . .

Mauá was the first who applied on a large scale in Brazil the joint stock company, who used the stock exchange in Rio and abroad (foremost that of London) for his purposes. A description of the crisis of 1875 (the result or the cause of Mauá's tragedy?) emphasizes that "a large part of the wealth of our city consists in valuable shares of companies' stock."

He understood how to absorb the available money of the country. The deposits of the Banco Mauá in the year 1857 amounted to 47,703 *contos de reis,* when the total of the issued paper money was 118,498 contos. His *vale* [chit] was the most popular; his influence on the exchange, immense.

The first ship in Amazonas, the first railroad to Petrópolis, the São Paulo railway, were products of the initiative of this great gaucho. The first locomotive used to be called *Baroneza* in honor of his wife.

He introduced the horse-car in Montevideo, participated in similar enterprises in Brussels and Lisbon, and was connected with this undertaking in Paris.

As a result of several reorganizations, Casa Mauá owned banks in Montevideo, in Buenos Aires, in Manchester, in London (Carruthers, de Castro & Co.), in New York (Carruthers, Dixon & Co.) and in nine cities of Brazil.

Mauá's activity had no geographical limits. He transformed economically the whole Atlantic coast—from Amazonas to La Plata. His penetration into the La Plata region is one of the most exciting chapters in the history of Brazilian foreign policy. He reorganized (1857) his agency in Montevideo into the Banco Mauá y Cia., the first bank in Montevideo, later an issue bank on a gold basis. He was a great *estanciero* in Uruguay, organized factories, introduced gas and the telegraph. At the Universal Exhibition of 1862 in London he was an exponent of Brazil, but he exhibited Uruguayan industries too. A railroad to Mato Grosso was, for him, a way for economic penetration into Paraguay and Bolivia, as was the opening of the Amazon to the steamship.

But Mauá's dream was "a Brazilian influence on European markets." His enterprises and interests were represented in Europe and in the United States of America.

Mauá was a member of Congress, he was a diplomat; as early as 1850, he organized, for the Visconde do Uruguay, the policy of intervention in Uruguay; he interceded again in 1864; he was the financier of the Paraguayan War (1865–1870).

The general opinion in the neighboring states was that "the Banco Mauá was the most powerful diplomatic agency of the Empire," as the president of the Banco do Uruguay (ex-president of the Republic) Dr. Claudio Williman expressed it. "The Brazilian Peril" was Mauá's name in La Plata.

Mauá's career was long. He survived the series of Brazilian crises in the third quarter of the century. Even the famous "Crise de Setembro" in 1864, when "Souto quebrou" did not influence his position.

The end of this striking career (1875) was deplorable. The old Visconde de Mauá had to earn his living in a small exchange brokerage. After the collapse of his bank, his creditors did not lose very much. They received 65 percent at the end of three years (1878) and on complete liquidation their dividend amounted to 94.7 percent (1882). "This result was, perhaps, unique in the history of bankruptcies in Brazil, unique certainly in the history of bank failures in Brazil." And this unique result was achieved in spite of the general crisis in the country for, besides special causes, Mauá's failure was a part of the series of financial tragedies of that time since both the Banco Allemão and the Banco Nacional shared his fate.

The importance of Mauá's activity in the Brazilian economic development is clear: he moved the frontier rapidly. Roads and railways imply docks and wharves, and once the railways start, the great era of "public works," which transforms a colony, begins. The development of means of communication resulted in a new penetration into the interior, in the adjustment of new areas. It was the first time in Brazilian history that technological progress of the country had been instigated by a business enthusiast. And this progress was not limited to the coast. Amazonas and Mato Grosso felt the pressure of Mauá's activity perhaps even more definitely than Rio de Janeiro and São Paulo. But he brought movement everywhere. There was no limit to his interest and initiative.

[His biographer] Faria gives a geographical résumé of Mauá's work, which shows his influence in moving the economic frontier:

> It was impossible to travel from the extreme north, to the extreme south, anywhere in the country without finding, on every turn, a work of his constructed through his genius: He practically discovered Amazonas, cutting through the great wasted waters, opening up vast forests to civilization by a navigation line of 3200 miles that astonished the learned Agassiz and his wife in 1865 on account of the order, the discipline, the cleanliness of the steamers, calling to mind the comfort of their museum at Cambridge; Rio Grande do Sul, glorious land of his birth, was also made accessible by him to overseas traffic, inaugurating direct commerce with Europe, cutting through the sand banks, removing the sand, in 1847, by means of his strong tug boats; in the middle of the country, the first railroads—the first five railroads —to the north, the two which reached from the captaincies of Pernambucco and Bahia toward the São Francisco, to the south, the three that crossed the Serra do Mar, which were, like that of Petrópolis and that of Santos to Jundiaí, his exclusive work—the former ones being his work coördinated with others, i.e., the D. Pedro II railroad company. Everywhere material improvements, progress, gas in Rio de Janeiro and in other cities, the Mangue Canal, the modern tanneries, the textile mills, the foundry and the shipyard in Niteroi, the sugar refining mills, the urban and maritime means of transportation, the foreign colonization, our industrial civilization, in short.

❧4❧

E. de Castro Rebello

Viscount Mauá
Viewed More Skeptically

*In reaction to the glorification of Mauá, Edgardo
de Castro Rebello, a young law student, sharply
criticized the work of Alberto de Faria. By-passing
the question of Mauá's contribution to Brazilian
growth, he concentrated his attention on the causes of
the viscount's success, the motives that impelled him,
and his hypocritical advocacy of free enterprise while
depending on government aid at every step.*

The name Mauá had already filled the entrepreneurial and
financial history of the country. The vestiges of his passage through the imperial Parliament had not been ob-
literated. He had thus acquired a place in the nation's history. But his biographer thought such place insufficient. He
desired to enlarge it, enlarge it and put it on a higher—in
fact, the highest—plane. From this desire emerges this
story of the "self-made man," who, thanks to individual
merit almost without equal, lifted himself far above his

Translated from E. de Castro Rebello, *Mauá, restaurando a verdade*
(Rio de Janeiro: Universo, 1932), pp. 10–20, 31–35. Copyright,
1932, by Edgardo de Castro Rebello. Translated and printed by
permission of the author.

contemporaries, . . . acquiring by hard work, intelligence, and probity a great fortune, political position, admiration, esteem, and respect. He is characterized as being idealistic, detached, self-denying, as consecrating his all to the service of two peoples—two native countries, almost—with the disinterest of the pure; finally, in the hour of adversity bearing everything heroically. Yesterday, a poor orphan; today, a modest clerk in a business firm; tomorrow, administrator of a large-scale establishment; later, a partner of his former boss, untiring entrepreneur, banker, deputy, baron, viscount, intrepid fighter against the most important politicians, friend of the leading figures of his day, underwriter of the nation's credit, which was surpassed by his own, builder of the nationality itself; envied even by the monarch, he becomes in the end the victim of the injustice and ingratitude of two nations. Such is the portrait of Mauá from the pen of his biographer. This work of special pleading, an unconditional apologia of individualism of which Mauá was, according to the author, "the great exponent in Brazil," belongs to one of the worst types of history—eulogistic history.

The biographer romanticizes Mauá's [early] life . . . ; but tells us nothing regarding the essentials that might allow us to form a more or less exact idea of the nature of Mauá's ascendance—the social condition of his parents, for example—and thus enable us to explain his fate. The fact that we then had a system of slave labor and that Mauá was not born a slave, as well as his having a maternal uncle who was a ship's captain, seem to be evidence enough to discard the hypothesis that his social origin was a mean one. In those days, being placed in a small business establishment and being subjected to the rigors of work as a clerk was not done because of *need*. Rather, this was the best—perhaps the only—manner of preparing a future businessman: apprenticeship was the indispensable school. Even today such practice is traditional in a large part of the commercial world.

The employment of Mauá by Carruthers' firm, his successive promotions to the position of manager and later to that of partner and the acquisition of a considerable fortune are facts that denote the possession of superior qualities. They are facts that make him exemplify those men who, because of their intelligence, ability, energy, if not because of lesser qualities, are able to triumph over life's difficulties. These successes would be impossible, however, without the contribution of *chance,* which his biographer conceals in the realm of legend. Such things as his ancestry, the beneficent hand extended by his maternal uncle to this orphan nephew, and, above all, the circumstance of his first employer having among his creditors the Englishman Carruthers in addition to the fact that Carruthers later wanted to retire to his native country leaving someone whom he could trust to direct his business are all factors which are not considered. . . .

For Alberto de Faria, Mauá's destiny begins to unfold when the blockade of the port of Buenos Aires, which the English and French had maintained, is terminated. The imperial [Brazilian] government resolved in 1850 to come to the defense of the besieged city of Montevideo. . . . The Brazilian government also began to lend pecuniary aid to the besieged forces when the French government reduced its subsidies.

What then happened is quite interesting, not because it uncovers a patriotic streak—a trace of self-abnegation —in the life of Mauá, but because, once again, it reveals the intimacy that exists everywhere among the capitalist states and men of finance, especially when what is under consideration is how to pay for a war. Mauá, who was still merely the businessman Irineu Evangelista de Souza, obliged himself by contract, subscribed to as well by Andrés Lamas, the representative of the government of the Banda Oriental [Uruguay], and, on the part of the Brazilian government, by the minister of finance, Rodrigues Torres (viscount of Itaboraí), to furnish the funds necessary for the defense of Montevideo and the struggle against the besiegers. . . . This *deal* into which Mauá plunged himself "body and soul" is described by Alberto de Faria as volunteering—for he was so noble—"to defend the cause of the besieged in the midst of innumerable risks. . . ."

Now let us tell the story as it should be told. At the age of thirty-six Mauá was "enormously rich"; his fortune was estimated at £300,000 sterling. Twenty-seven years later he himself was to say to his creditors that at the time of the above-mentioned adventure the "surplus" of his "personal assets" allowed him to "cover any unforeseen circumstances." Where, then, was the altruism? This was merely business. In lending money for the war, he did nothing more than invest it—that is, the "surplus"—without any risk to himself, at the very time that the imperial government was throwing its military strength into service for the same cause, thus sacrificing the lives of numerous Brazilians. . . .

The connections between Mauá and the political leaders of that period were well known. During his youth it was principally the Conservative Party that was dominant. His connections were, therefore, preferably with the leaders of that party: Paraná, Mont'Alegre, Uruguai, Itaboraí, Eusébio. These friendships were so close that . . . he was once publicly accused of having been involved in the repression of the Liberal Revolution of Minas (1842). In 1850 the first contract was signed by which Mauá gave monetary aid to [Brazil's ally] the Montevideo government. The following year Mauá, along with others, obtained a government concession for working the silver and copper mines in the provinces of São Pedro [Rio Grande do Sul] and Santa Catarina. In the same year he received from the same cabinet a concession for the establishment of a gaslighting system in the city of Rio de Janeiro. The following year the imperial government granted him the exclusive privilege during thirty years for the navigation of the Amazon River. In 1856, he and others were authorized to create a company that was charged with constructing, using, and financing a railroad between Santos and Jundiaí. In 1858, he was given the contract for building the Mangue Canal. The provincial government of Rio de Janeiro gave him the concession for constructing and exploiting a railroad from Estrela to the foot of the *serra* [escarpment] of Petrópolis; and the federal government a concession to establish a ferry between the city of Rio and the port of Estrela.

Alberto de Faria exalts the advantages that, according to him, the government obtained upon making these concessions. As to those related to the lighting system, for example, he repeats—as he does concerning nearly every topic—what Mauá himself had said: that by preferring his offer to that of one of his competitors, the government saved 12,000 *contos de reis;* the truth is that this same deal allowed Mauá to pocket nearly £250,000, which at that time was a prodigious sum. For construction of the Mangue Canal he received nearly 1,400 *contos de reis.* . . . The value of the favors granted Mauá can be measured by the terms of the concession by which the company he organized was led to provide shipping in the Amazon: exclusive privilege for thirty years; an annual subsidy of 160 *contos de reis* for fifteen years for the first line; and a sliding scale subsidy . . . for the second not to be less than 40 *contos de reis* per year. The annual dividends which the company distributed to the stockholders reached 12 percent. . . .

In the lecture that preceded the publication of his great book, he [Faria] had told us . . . that . . . the establishment of [an iron foundry and shipyard at] Ponta d'Areia "came to be the central pillar of our industrial grandeur." [He partly explains its creation by] . . . a chance occurrence, a visit to industrial Bristol. [But] . . . there is one question that it in itself does not resolve: to what kind of influences might Mauá have succumbed when he abandoned the branch of business in which he had become rich in order to become, rather, an industrialist and banker? For his biographer, Mauá is a man whose life borders on the supernatural when it does not actually go beyond it. In order that, in 1846 or 1847, he would decide to leave "a prosperous business, which had made so many persons rich and which seemed to be growing steadily," he must have been impelled by some less mundane purpose.

"What religious or philosophical wind made this business-man into an apostle?" His biographer asks this question and answers it with certainty: "Mauá is doubtless among those in the past century who were influenced by the sociological ideas of Henri de Saint-Simon. . . ."

The truth is that in all this there is much imagination. The establishment of Ponta d'Areia is a prosaic story. In the first place, we must not forget that the modest shed he purchased already covered both industries: the iron foundry and naval construction. The original owner, who probably never had a "day in Bristol" in his life, had associated them intuitively. Mauá did nothing more than follow in that man's footsteps, although, to be sure, he developed both businesses on a much larger scale.

Another point that occurs to everyone is this: five years lapsed between the first voyage of Mauá to Europe and his purchase of the above-mentioned establishment. In addition, even after his visit to Bristol, Mauá sought to enlarge the scope of his former business by convincing Carruthers to found a branch in Manchester. The point is that all this happened before 1844. The tariff system that Alves Branco, then minister of finance, inaugurated in that year to provide a policy of strict protection—for some people truly prohibitive—was not merely an "aid" for the Ponta d'Areia foundry during more than ten years; it was the condition that determined its existence and prosperity. Why not admit that it could well have been the motive for Mauá's terminating his former business?

Why, then, complicate what is so simple? Unless some undiscovered document exists that would prove the existence of some influence in Mauá's life of the sociological school of Henri de Saint-Simon, the affirmation of such a link is entirely gratuitous.

Mary Wilhelmine Williams

Negro Slavery in Brazil: Benevolent and Humane

The commonly accepted view of slavery in Brazil is that it was characterized by personal ties of affection between master and slave and was much less oppressive than in the United States. This view is here pointedly presented by Miss Mary Wilhelmine Williams (1878–1944), the biographer of Pedro II, who was for many years Professor of History at Goucher College.

. . . The lot of the Brazilian slaves was rather better than that of their fellow bondmen in the United States. Three most important factors bearing upon the subject remain to be considered; and these should not only remove all question regarding the relative positions of the Brazilian Empire and the North American Union with reference to the matter under consideration, but should lend strong support to the view that the Brazilians treated their African bondmen better, on the whole, than any other nation.

From Mary Wilhelmine Williams, "The Treatment of Negro Slaves in the Brazilian Empire: A Comparison with the United States of America," *The Journal of Negro History*, XV (July 1930), 315–336. These excerpts are from pp. 329–336. Reprinted by permission of the Association for the Study of Negro Life and History, Inc.

One of the factors was the unifying influence of the Roman Catholic Church, with which the casual and diminishing part played by the Protestant groups in the Southern United States offers no comparison. At a very early period it became customary to baptize all Negroes from the Portuguese colony of Angola before placing them on the slave ships; and the law required that all other slaves be taught certain prayers and be baptized within a year after arrival from Africa. Though many masters complied with this requirement rather tardily, they rarely evaded it completely, for to do so was in opposition to public opinion. . . . Children of slaves were usually christened promptly after birth, taught the catechism like the children of the free, and in due time, were received in full membership into the Church.

After this, they regularly went to mass and confession, and partook of the sacrament; for all of the large plantations were supplied with chapels and priests. Like the free, they had religious societies, which they themselves officered; and pious slaves gladly contributed of their savings towards the decoration of images of the saints. And, finally, the law required that when the slave's earthly labors were ended he be buried, like his white master, in consecrated ground.

But church membership not only classed the Negro as a living soul capable of salvation. It gave him in the priest a counselor whose influence was largely for the good, and a friend to whom he could appeal for protection against injustice; for the kindness of the Brazilian clergy to their own slaves was proverbial. Most important of all—and most difficult fully to evaluate because the influence was so subtle—membership in the Roman Church bound the slaves with all the power represented by that organization to white Brazilians in a brotherhood based upon the recognition of God as the common father. . . .

The most striking difference between the attitude in

Brazil towards the Negro slaves and that in the United States was the ease with which the bondmen could, in the former country, secure manumission. Whereas, in most of the slave-holding states of the North American Union emancipation was either discouraged or absolutely prohibited by law, because of the ever present fear of the free black, in Brazil it was stimulated and facilitated to a degree unparalleled elsewhere in the history of Negro slavery. The source of this attitude appears to have been less governmental action than public opinion, which crystallized into custom having almost the weight of law.

Faithful nurses usually received their freedom after a time, and slave mothers were often given their liberty when they had borne ten children. As a deed of piety, well-to-do masters oftener than not emancipated some or all of their slaves in their wills. Such action was strongly fostered by the clergy, who were themselves much given to manumission. The slight commercial value of very young infants also frequently resulted in their emancipation, for custom demanded that the owner liberate them if their market price was offered him at the time of their baptism. They were perhaps oftenest freed by their fathers, if the latter were themselves free, but there was also a strong tradition stimulating godparents to this generous act, and slave mothers, consequently, were at times shrewd enough to choose sponsors for their children from the benevolent well-to-do.

According to a host of authors, Brazilian law required that a master emancipate his slave if the latter could pay his market price and desired his liberty, but the present writer failed to find trace of any such document after careful search through the available Portuguese and Brazilian legal collections, and she is, therefore, inclined to believe that long established custom was mistaken for law, even by many Brazilians who, accordingly, misled foreign travelers interested in the question. This view is supported by Christie, who, in the middle of the last century, made a special study in Brazil of slavery and the slave-trade. He definitely states that the idea was a mistake, for no such law existed. And Handelmann also says that manumission under the conditions mentioned was produced by custom maintained by common consent, and not by law.

Whether or not such a law was written among the statutes of Brazil is of little importance to the question under consideration, for beyond a doubt it was a very common practice in Brazil for masters to emancipate slaves who requested their freedom and could supply the purchase money. Manumission continually took place as a result of its influence, especially among the *Negros de ganho,* who had the best opportunities to earn and save money. Stevedores and other carriers could, on good days, make even six or eight times as much money as their masters required as their portion, and some were thus able to buy themselves free in two or three years. Sometimes a group of such men would club together and buy the freedom of a favorite friend; but the Minas coffee-carriers also organized in groups under a captain and labored for the freedom of all. The order in which they should secure their liberty was generally determined by casting lots, but it appears to have been customary for those earliest liberated to remain by the group and labor until the last slave was his own man. Large numbers of the Minas in this manner purchased their freedom, after which they usually returned to Africa, paying their passage with the surplus they had acquired.

Even slaves who received no money from their masters were at times able to free themselves, because they had the many religious feast days of the Roman Catholic Church as well as all Sundays in which to work for themselves; and, unlike the enslaved Negroes in the United States, were permitted to engage freely in commercial activities in their own interest. Hence, some of them grew and marketed cotton and other produce on the little plots of ground which they often had for their own on the plantations. Others earned through plaiting and selling baskets and other articles from straw, or through the disposal of vessels and utensils fashioned from gourds and calabashes, and known as "God's earthenware."

While it is quite true that occasionally masters refused flatly to sell their slaves the freedom which the latter were capable of purchasing, it is also a fact that Negroes who might have had their liberty for the asking preferred to remain in slavery because they possessed good masters, and to them the advantages of freedom seemed too problematical to experiment with; for, if they returned to Africa as freemen, there was always danger until after 1853 of being recaptured by slavers; while, if they remained in Brazil, they were liable to military service, from which, as slaves, they were exempt; and, if they escaped the army, there was always the possibility that as freemen the competition of others might defeat their efforts even to make a living.

The readiness with which the Brazilians emancipated their Negroes is best explainable by the third, and last, factor to be considered as fundamentally differentiating slavery conditions in the Brazilian Empire from those in the United States—the fact that the Brazilians, in common with the Portuguese and Spaniards, felt practically no color prejudice towards people of Ethiopian blood. While the southerners from the United States—particularly during the latter part of the slavery era—argued that the Negro was a mere superbrute, having little in common with the white man, and foredoomed by nature through racial and cultural inferiority to permanent servitude of the superior race, the Brazilians recognized the manhood of the enslaved blacks and saw in them potentiality for progress and for ultimate cultural equality with the whites; and, as a result, gave the Negroes, whether bound or free, greater opportunities for advancement than they anywhere else enjoyed.

The difference in viewpoint is best shown by a comparison of the lot of the free Negroes in the two countries. Whereas, in the United States, because their presence was regarded as a menace to slavery as an institution, and to the cultural standards of the land, the free blacks were very few in number, and were so restricted by law and custom as to be free in little but name, in Brazil they had all of the rights of white men. There was no discrimination of color, which fact made Brazil, as a southern white woman resident there put it, "the very paradise of the Negroes." By marriage they mixed freely with the whites of their own social class, and no racial barrier discouraged the development of their talents. To them all trades and professions were open, and the realms of art and scholarship, as well; political offices were held by ex-slaves and the children of ex-slaves; and, as priests, they ministered to white as well as black, and were even raised to bishoprics in the Roman Catholic Church.

Partly as a result of the unusual opportunities given the Brazilian Negro for self-development under slavery, partly because, once emancipated, no door which his character and abilities qualified him to enter was barred to him, the free Negro early made good. The free blacks constituted no special problem or menace, such as existed in the United States. Accordingly, the inclination to manumit was stimulated, rather than discouraged by their presence, with the result that very early the whites of Brazil were quite outnumbered by free blacks; and before slavery had been completely abolished many Negroes had risen to positions of prominence. The emancipation of more than six hundred thousand Negro slaves in 1888 without a serious shock to the social structure was made possible by the presence of this great body of free, colored Brazilians. . . .

6

Stanley J. Stein

Negro Slavery in Brazil: Harsh and Cruel

Professor Stanley J. Stein of Princeton University presents a sharply revisionist view of slavery in Brazil in his well-documented study of a coffee county near Rio de Janeiro. It is possible that this area—which was virtually unpopulated in colonial times—differed from that of the old sugar plantations of the northeast, where slaves institutions were older. But of course slavery, when seen in terms of specific situations, is never pleasant.

. . . Constant supervision and thorough control through discipline joined to swift, often brutal punishment were considered an absolute necessity on coffee plantations. Proper functioning of a *fazenda* varied directly with the steady application of the working force; in an epoch of little machinery, slave labor or what Brazilians termed "organized labor," had to be guided carefully and supervised closely. . . .

Reprinted by permission of the publishers from Stanley J. Stein, *Vassouras: A Brazilian Coffee County, 1850–1900* (Cambridge, Mass.: Harvard University Press, 1957), pp. 132–139.

In their reasoning, the needs of production dovetailed with concepts of slave character. "Only with constantly exercised vigilance under military-like discipline" would slaves work hard and earnestly, was a widespread opinion. The Negro slave was "by nature the enemy of all regular work," the "passive partner" in the transaction that entrusted him to his owner at the time of purchase. His salary? The purchase price and food and clothing provided by his master. . . .

A description of a Paraíba Valley planter published shortly before the abolition of slavery, underscores the prevalence of prejudices, the effect of routinism, and the absence of scientific knowledge. Though a planter might be capable of displaying compassion and pity for whites, toward his slaves he was "harsh and very cruel" for he refused to see in them the "nature and dignity" of men. The slave was little more than an "animated object, a tool, an instrument, a machine."

On isolated fazendas, amid numerous slaves, planters perceived the precariousness of their situation. Many declared openly "The slave is our uncompromising enemy." And the enemy had to be restrained and kept working on schedule through fear of punishment, by vigilance and discipline, by forcing him to sleep in locked quarters, by prohibiting communication with slaves of nearby fazendas, and by removing all arms from his possession. Where *fazendeiros* judged that one of their number did not maintain adequate firmness toward his slaves, they applied pressure, direct or indirect. Manoel de Azevedo Ramos discovered this when he brought charges against the overseer of a nearby plantation for beating unmercifully one of his slaves. Neighbors testified that Azevedo Ramos enforced little discipline on his establishment, and the case was dropped since witnesses refused to testify in his behalf. To judge by tasks assigned him, the model planter was an omnipotent, omnipresent, beneficent despot, a father to his "flock" of slaves when they were obedient and resigned, a fierce and vengeful lord when transgressed. And, unlike the urban slaveholder whose punishments were somewhat regulated by law, "on the fazendas of the interior the master's will decided and the drivers carried it out." Lightest of punishments might be the threat "Mend your ways or I'll send you to the Cantagallo slave market," more serious might be the age-old instruments of corporal punishment.

Most visible symbol of the master's authority over the slave, the whip enjoyed several names: there was the literate term *chicote* for what was usually a five-tailed and metal-tipped lash, colloquially known as the "codfish" or "armadillo tail." Probably because Portuguese drivers went armed with such cat-o'-nine-tails, slaves tagged it with the name of the favorite article of Portuguese diet—codfish. It was felt that sometimes it was used too much, sometimes too little, for often masters had the "very poor habit of failing to whip on the spot, and prefer to threaten the vexatious slave with 'Wait, you'll pay for this all at once' or 'The cup is brimming, wait 'til it pours over and *then* we'll see'—and at that time they grab and beat him unmercifully; why? because he paid for his misdeeds *all at once!!!!*" It was difficult to apply legal restraints to the planters' use of the lash. When one of the founding fathers of Vassouras, Ambrozio de Souza Coutinho, proposed, as one of the municipal regulations of 1829, that "Every master who mistreats his slaves with blows and lashes, with repeated and inhuman punishment proven by verbal testimony . . ." be fined, fellow-planters refused to accept it. Not sheer perversity but the desire to drive slaves to work longer and harder motivated liberal use of the lash. "Many inhuman fazendeiros," wrote Caetano da Fonseca, more than thirty years after Souza Coutinho, "force their slaves with the lash to work beyond physical endurance. These wretched slaves, using up their last drops of energy, end

their days in a brief time." And, he added, "with great
financial damage to their barbarous masters." Indeed there
were masters who believed "their greatest happiness was
to be considered skillful administrators, men who force
from their slaves the greatest amount of work with the
smallest possible expense."

Whipping was not done by the *senhor* himself who "ordered his overseer to beat the slaves." The whipping over,
overseers rubbed on the open wounds a "mixture of pepper,
salt and vinegar," probably as a cauterizer but interpreted
by slaves as "to make it hurt more." An ingenious labor-
saving variation of the whip was reported by ex-slaves.
This was a water-driven "codfish" by which a whip secured
to a revolving water-wheel lashed slaves tied to a bench.
So widespread was use of the lash, that terms such as "ful-
minating apoplexy" and "cerebral congestion" were employed as medical explanation for death induced by whipping. Typical is an eye-witness account of a beating told
by an ex-slave. On orders from the master, two drivers
bound and beat a slave while the slave folk stood in line,
free folk watching from further back. The slave died that
night and his corpse, dumped into a wicker basket, was
borne by night to the slave cemetery of the plantation and
dropped into a hastily dug grave. "Slaves could not com-
plain to the police; only another fazendeiro could do that,"
explained the eye-witness.

Only slightly less brutal than the whippings were the
hours spent by male and female slaves alike in the *tronco,*
a form of heavy iron stock common on plantations. Arms
and legs were imprisoned together forcing the victim to sit
hunched forward with arms next to ankles, or to lie on
one side. This was the *tronco duplo;* the *tronco simples*
merely imprisoned legs. One ex-slave claimed that she had
been told that the fazendeiro placed her to her mother's
breast to nurse while her mother served her punishment in
a *tronco duplo.* Another variation was the long wooden

stock (*tronco de pau comprido*) into which were locked the feet of four or five slaves. For inveterate offenders an iron hook or collar (*gancho*) was used to encircle the neck. For less important offenses the slave's open palm was slapped with a hardwood palm-slapper (*palmatorio*). Inveterate runaways were chained to each other and put into field gangs, or forced to wear a heavy iron weight on one foot. Such chain gangs were part of the *pena de gales* prescribed by the Imperial Criminal Code of 1830. This form of punishment may have inspired the jongo:

> Pretty little canary, kept in a cage
> Why the little chain on your leg, please tell why?

The worst offender of all was the unregenerate, rebellious slave. If the planter did not kill him outright, he wisely preferred to sell him away. . . . Zeferina Adelaide das Chagas Werneck sold an African slave south to Rio Grande do Sul because "it is necessary to remove him from the fazenda and to sell him because he is insubordinate and will not work and he may serve as a bad example to the other slaves."

As a complement to supervision, to discipline, and to fear of corporal punishment, fazendeiros hoped that the local priest, on visits to plantations of his parish, would use the sermon to "rehabilitate the Negro's condition, to consecrate his relations with his master, who would thereby no longer appear as proprietor or tyrant but rather as father, as a portrait of God, whom he should love and serve with the sacrifice of his toil and sweat." The Barão do Paty suggested that the conscientious confessor instil in the slave "love for work and blind obedience to his masters and to those who control him." Such an attitude other Vassouras planters expressed laconically as "religion is a restraining force and teaches resignation" and therefore planters should "push by every means the development

of religious ideas." Planters were not to quibble over the
costs of the visiting priest, for "in addition to being necessary for the good, the spiritual grazing of souls, such
expenses contribute heavily to maintain the morality, order,
submission and proper discipline of . . . slaves who cannot be kept in hand and controlled merely by temporal
punishment." Padre Caetano da Fonseca advised that "confession is the antidote of slave insurrections," that the
confessor was to teach the slave to see in the master a
father and therefore owed him "love, respect and obedience." Through the confessor, explained this priest, the
slave learned that "this life is as nothing compared to
eternity" and that "the slave who bears his captivity pa-
tiently finds recompense in the heavenly kingdom where
all are equal before God." . . .

In a society, half free and half slave, many Vassouras
planters maintained harmonious relations with the individual members of their labor force. Strong attachments based
upon affection and mutual respect often obscured the harsh
reality of slavery. A notable difference developed between
the affluent planters and the proprietors of small holdings
with regard to this relationship. While the large planter
had to employ intermediaries to direct the activities of
his labor force, the *sitiante* directed his few field hands personally, resided in unpretentious quarters hardly better than
those of his slaves, even "maintained his slaves as part of
his family and fed them on the same fare." . . .

7

Joaquim Nabuco

◆━◆◉◆━◆

Negro Slavery in Brazil: The Chief Obstacle to Development

Joaquim Nabuco (1849–1910) was one of the ablest leaders of the abolitionist movement that culminated in the end of Brazilian slavery in 1888. Although he was often willing to play upon humanitarian feelings by emphasizing the cruelties of slavery, his chief emphasis was upon the retarding, unprogressive influence of that institution. He appealed to those urban interests committed to the transformation of Brazil. His references to the possibility of making slaves into active consumers are especially pointed. He also counted on the very human tendency to find a single cause for the myriad troubles that beset Brazilian society; if only this major social reorganization were carried out, Brazil would become a progressive, industrial nation with a prosperous agricultural class of small landowners.

In 1880 the Provincial Assembly of [the province of] Rio de Janeiro sent a communication to the General Assembly in which the following passage appears:

Translated from Joaquim Nabuco, *O abolicionismo* (London: Kingdon, 1883), pp. 147–155, 160–167, 179–185.

The picture that presents itself to the view of one who traverses the interior of the province is a desolate one. Especially precarious is the situation in the counties in the tidewater region where the primeval fertility of the soil has been exhausted and where neglect has caused the fertile valleys to be transformed into deep stagnant lakes, which make faint those who approach. The unfortunate inhabitants of the countryside, without leadership, support, or examples to follow, are not part of the social community; they neither consume nor produce. . . .

These words from a slaveholding assembly describe the effects of slavery: wherever it goes it burns the forests, mines and depletes the soil; and, when it pulls up stakes, it leaves behind a devastated country in which vegetates a wretched population of nomadic proletarians. What happens in Rio de Janeiro occurs in all the other provinces where slavery has been implanted. . . .

The truth is that the vast regions exploited by colonial slavery have a uniform appearance of sadness and abandonment: there is in them neither the union of man and land, nor the indications of permanent habitation, nor the signs of natural growth. The past is visible, but there is no sign of a future. The present is the gradual wasting away that foretells death.

The population does not definitively possess the soil. The large landholder conquered it from nature with his slaves, exploited it, and made himself wealthy by exhausting it; later he went bankrupt because of the extravagant uses to which unscrupulously acquired fortunes are put; and, finally, he returned this soil to Mother Nature, spoiled and exhausted. . . .

The final result of this system is the poverty and misery of the country. Nor is it surprising that the cultivation of the soil by a class without any interest in the work that is extorted from it should have these results. As we know, land tenure under a slave system consists in the division of all the cultivated land into a certain number of huge properties. . . . The division of a vast province into veritable penal colonies, small Ashantis [African kingdoms] in which only one will rules . . . serves to obstruct progress. It cannot bring about any permanent benefit to the region so divided up or to the free population that lives in it in a state of continual dependence upon the grace of the landowners. For this very reason progress in the interior is nil, even after 300 years of national existence. . . .

What is observed in the north is also seen in the south and would be even more apparent if coffee were dethroned by the *Hemyleia Vastatrix* [a coffee blight]. During the golden age of sugar, the north presented an appearance that deluded many. The houses, the so-called *palacetes* of the territorial aristocracy in Bahia and Recife, the liveries of the footmen, the litters, the sedan chairs, and the noble carriages are vestiges of the once-flourishing monopoly of sugar cane—before the sugar beet appeared on the horizon. Likewise the wealth of southern agriculture—in fact much exaggerated and difficult to liquidate but, nevertheless, considerable and, in some cases, huge for this country—represents the temporary prosperity of coffee. Competition will arise as it did for sugar. . . . When the reign of coffee is over (and low prices are already a forecast), the south will be reduced to the same condition as the north. . . . Look at Rio de Janeiro and Minas Gerais: without coffee they are two decrepit provinces. . . .

São Paulo is a special case. In spite of its being the current bastion of slavery, in São Paulo and in the provinces of the south it has not caused such great ruin. São Paulo has employed a great part of its capital in the purchase of slaves from the north, but its agriculture does not depend as much on slavery for its solvency as does that of Rio de Janeiro and Minas Gerais. *Paulista* initiative has been much exaggerated in recent years because the province, after seeing the results of the railroad from Santos to Jundiaí, has built railways without aid from the national government. The *Paulistas* are not, as they have been called, the Yankees of Brazil (which has no Yankees); neither is São Paulo the most advanced province, nor the most American, nor the most liberal in spirit in the country. It would be the Louisiana of Brazil, not the Massachusetts. Still, it is true that the province, for having entered into its period of prosperity at the end of the reign of slavery, will show greater elasticity in the crisis than its [northern] neighbors.

In Paraná, Santa Catarina, and Rio Grande [do Sul], European immigration infuses new blood into the veins of the populace. Immigrants react against slavery, and the newness of the land and the temperate climate open greater horizons to free labor than to slavery. . . .

The illusion of wealth, of national development . . . does not fool anyone who examines its shadows. [Our] reality is that of a people that is more slave than master of the vast territory it occupies; a people in whose eyes work has been systematically debased and to whom it has been taught that nobility consists of making others work; a people that is stranger to the school; a people indifferent to all those feelings, instincts, desires, and necessities that make the inhabitants of a single country not simply a society, but a nation. When Sr. Silveira Martins told the Senate that "Brazil is coffee and coffee is the Negro"— not wishing, of course, to say slave—he defined Brazil as a plantation, a commercial enterprise dominated by a small minority of vested interests, in short, today's slaveholding Brazil. But it is enough that a country populated by more than 10 million inhabitants, vaster than European Russia, almost twice the size of Europe without Russia, and more than a third the size of the British Empire on five continents be described in such a manner in order to evaluate what slavery has done to it. . . .

The influence of slavery on the land and on the population that lives from it was disastrous in every sense of the word. . . . The characteristics of the slave system are improvidence, routine methods, lack of interest in using machines, disdain for future interests, and ambition to obtain the greatest possible profit with the least possible work on one's own part regardless of the extent of damage to future generations. The feudal division of the land, which slavery instituted, along with the labor monopoly that it created, impedes the formation of nucleuses of industrial workers and the extension of commerce to the interior.

In every sense, slavery was and is an obstacle to the material development of the counties; the land was exploited without concern for the locality and without recognition of obligations to the people outside one's doors. Burning, planting, abandoning. The profits consumed through the purchase of slaves and in the luxuries of the city. No one to build schools, churches, bridges, canals, or riverworks. No one to found asylums, or to construct roads, or to build houses—not even for the slaves—or to encourage industry, or to increase the value of or make improvements on the land, or to till the soil, or to utilize machines, or to contribute in any way to the progress of the surrounding region. What slavery did do was to sterilize the soil through its extensive cultivation, brutalize the slaves, impede the development of the counties, and spread about the outskirts of the seignorial fiefs a miasmatic region devastated by the institutions it supported. . . .

Throughout the entire [free] population of the interior, whether on the fringes of the capital cities or in the treeless plateau of the *sertão,* its effects were: dependence; misery; ignorance; subjection to the arbitrary will of potentates (for whom [the threat of] forced recruitment in the army was the principal means of action); lack of a piece of land that the poor man could call his own, even to cultivate for a short time; want of a house, which might be for him an inviolable retreat from which he could not be driven out at will; absence of a respected and protected family. . . . These were the people that moved away from the coast, living like gypsies, sticking occasionally to the plantations where they found shelter, forming themselves into little nucleuses in the interstices of the agricultural holdings, building their four mud walls where they were given permission to do so in exchange for conditions of vassalage that made the resident workers into mere serfs. Wherever one might look the effects were the same. *Latifundia perdidere Italiam* is a living truth to Brazilians. . . .

There are still other classes whose development is retarded by slavery: the laborers, the industrialists, and, in general, the commercial classes. Slavery does not permit the rise of real industrial workers, nor is it compatible with a wage system and the personal dignity of the artisan. The artisan, in order not to be the object of the social stigma that slavery imposes on its workers, tries to make clear the distance that separates him from the slave and thus imbues himself with a feeling of superiority, which is nothing more than meanness of soul on the part of one who escaped from slavery or is the son of slaves. Furthermore, working classes are not strong, respected, and intelligent in countries where those who employ workers are accustomed to ordering slaves around. Also, the workers do not exercise among us the smallest political influence.

Slavery and industry are always mutually exclusive terms just as are slavery and immigration. The spirit of slavery, spreading itself over a country, kills each one of the human faculties from which industry results: initiative, invention, individual energy. It stifles each of the elements that industry requires: accumulation of capital, abundance of labor, technical education of the workers, confidence in the future. . . .

In regard to commerce, slavery proceeds in this way:

because of mistrust reinforced by habit, commerce is shut off from the interior, that is, from all areas outside the provincial capitals except for Santos and Campinas in São Paulo, Petrópolis and Campos in Rio de Janeiro, Pelotas in Rio Grande do Sul, and a very few other cities. Stores carry only necessary articles, maintain small stocks of them, and what they sell is crude or adulterated. . . . Therefore, that which is not ordered directly from the capital is received by the consumer only through the peddler, whose story is the story of the civilization of our entire interior and who is, in fact, the commercial "pioneer" and represents the limits within which slavery is compatible with local exchange.

Commerce is, moreover, both the life source of slavery and its banker. In the past generation, it sustained bondage everywhere with [newly imported] Africans; many of the agricultural holdings fell into the hands of slave suppliers, and the fortunes acquired by the illicit slave trade . . . were, if not exported or converted into sumptuous buildings, employed in "aiding" agriculture through usury. In the current generation, the link between commerce and slavery . . . continues to be the same. The principal customers of commercial houses are slave owners. . . . Therefore, commercial activity in Brazil does not grow and does not open up new horizons for the country. Rather, it is an inactive force, without stimulus, fully aware that it is merely a prolongation of slavery. More correctly, it is the mechanism by which human flesh is converted into gold and circulated. . . .

As long as slavery persists, trade will always be the servant of a class, lacking independence. Commerce will never flourish in a system that does not allow it to enter into direct relations with consumers and that does not transform the population of the interior into consumers.

Of the classes that this system has artificially spawned the largest is that of public employees. . . . Thus, under the slave system, everything is expected to come from the state, which, being the only active organization, seeks and absorbs—through taxes and loans—all the available capital to distribute it among its clients by public employment. It sucks up the savings of the poor through inflation and makes the fortunes of the rich precarious. As a consequence, then, government employment has become the "noble profession" and the vocation of all. Take twenty or thirty Brazilians at random in any place where our elite gathers: all of them either are, or were, or will be civil servants; if not they, then their sons will be. . . . The class that thus lives with their eyes turned to the munificence of the government is extremely large and is the direct result of slavery, for having monopolized the land, degraded manual labor, and corrupted the feeling of personal pride into a disdain for whoever works in an inferior position or does not make others work, it does not allow Brazilians any other choice of career.

8

João Pandiá Calógeras

The Paraguayan War
as Seen by a Brazilian

The major international incident in South America
during the nineteenth century was the war waged by
Paraguay against Brazil, Argentina, and Uruguay.
Sometimes known as the War of the Triple Alliance,
it proved to be a watershed in Brazilian history. Bra-
zilians look back upon it as their great national war, a
substitute, in the formation of heroes, for the wars
of independence of the Spanish American republics.
It is still the subject of much controversy among his-
torians; here João Pandiá Calogeras (1870–1934),
businessman, economist, public servant, and writer,
presents the standard Brazilian interpretation.

. . . Though freed from the nightmare of absorption
by Rosas, the little republic of Uruguay was still torn by
the ambitions of rival factions of the *Blancos* and *Colorados* and for a number of years was a prey to an intolerable anarchy. During the space of the four years from
1852 to 1856, the unhappy country had been the victim

From João Pandiá Calógeras, *A History of Brazil*, trans. and ed.,
Percy Alvin Martin (Chapel Hill: University of North Carolina
Press, 1939), pp. 200–201, 208–209, 213–215. Reprinted by permis-
sion of the publisher.

of three revolutions, as many dictatorships, and two provisional executives. It is unnecessary to add that during these seemingly interminable struggles foreign interests were gravely jeopardized. Brazil, Uruguay's neighbor on the north, was the worst sufferer.

The imperial government was careful to show no preferences in these internal conflicts in Uruguay. It adhered to a strict neutrality and officially maintained diplomatic relations with the government in power at the time. This had also been true in an earlier period. The Brazilian authorities had treated successively with Rivera, Oribe, and the defenders of Montevideo as long as they wielded lawful authority. It is an absurdity to speak of such or such party as being the friends or protegés of Brazil. But in the distracted republic of Uruguay opinions ran quite the contrary. Each group in power begged for the Empire's assistance; and its sentiments toward its great northern neighbor depended on the extent to which such aid was forthcoming.

Thanks to the wider perspective and the greater knowledge at our disposal, these erroneous opinions are no longer held. With virtual unanimity, historians of the present day acknowledge that the real aims of Brazil were liberal and unselfish. Even those who in the past have criticised and censured the imperial policy in the Platine countries have recanted and generously avowed their mistakes. In recent years the Brazilian archives have been thrown open and confidential documents have been published. It is no longer possible to doubt the sincerity of the government of Rio, either in its pretensions or in its acts. . . .

. . . The elder López [Paraguayan dictator Carlos Antonio] died in 1862 and was succeeded by his son Francisco Solano [López]. It is exceedingly difficult to find anything good to say of this man. . . . The lives, the honor, the possessions of his subjects he looked upon as his own and disposed of them as suited his fancy. The slightest attempt at disobedience was visited with death. . . .

. . . History would seem to show that there is a kind of insanity, a delusion of greatness, if you will, which at some stage in their career, is apt to take possession of those entrusted with the destinies of people. In South America, Simón Bolívar harbored grandiose dreams of empire and in the end plowed the sea. On a smaller scale, Dom João VI and Dom Pedro I likewise nurtured imperialistic ambitions which finally came to naught. Rosas, the Argentine dictator, met the same fate. Now came Paraguay's turn. Everything points to López's ambition to erect a Greater Paraguay by absorbing the republic of Uruguay and the Argentine provinces of Entre Ríos and Corrientes. Thus would the little land-locked country become a great Atlantic power with Montevideo as its capital.

Such a program was indeed bold and daring and under certain conditions not entirely without the bounds of possibility. [But] to carry it out would entail the crushing of Uruguay, the dismemberment of Argentina, and possible hostilities with Brazil, whose interests would almost certainly be jeopardized. Only a political and military genius could hope to encompass such a task. Certainly Francisco Solano López was not such a genius. . . .

On November 11, 1864, the dictator López without warning . . . captured the Brazilian steamer *Marquês de Olinda* as it was leaving Asunción for the interior of Brazil, . . . [made a] prisoner [of] Colonel Carneiro de Campos, the new president of the province of Mato Grosso, and . . . seized various official documents, as well as remittances to the provincial treasury. The amazement of the Brazilians at this outrage was equaled only by their indignation. The entire country, without distinction of party or class, demanded that this affront to the national honor receive its just punishment.

Passions aroused by a seemingly gratuitous attack on national dignity render difficult an objective judgment of these events. But truth and equity demand that we make an honest attempt to fathom the motives of López at this time. In justifying his actions, the Paraguayan dictator alleged that the occupation of the Uruguayan town of Melo by the Brazilian troops in October, 1864, constituted for the Paraguayans a *casus belli*. Such a statement is absurd on two grounds. In the first place, the Brazilian-Uruguayan difficulties were no concern of López. Secondly, the occupation of Melo stood well within the legal activities of a campaign of reprisals being carried on by the imperial government against Uruguay, after all efforts at conciliation had broken down.

The truth of the matter is that López knew well what he was doing. He realized fully that the wanton seizure of the *Marquês de Olinda* would precipitate war with Brazil but he had, as he thought, counted the cost. And it must be owned that, if in the furtherance of his ambitious plans, he chose to throw down the gauntlet to the largest country of Hispanic America the moment was not ill-chosen. In Uruguay, he felt that he could count on the alliance of the *Blancos*; in Entre Ríos, that of Urquiza. As for Brazil itself, he hoped to make short work of its army. And in truth it must be said Paraguay was in a strong position. . . .

. . . Now that hostilities had actually broken out between Paraguay and Brazil, the formidable character of López's military machine became more evident. As early as November, 1864, he had 80,000 troops trained and equipped. A few months later this figure rose to 100,000. On the other hand, Brazil had only 17,000 troops; half were dispersed throughout the Empire, half fortunately, concentrated in the province of Rio Grande do Sul. The largest number Brazil ever had in the field during the whole course of the war was 68,000 (in April, 1866). It will be seen that this fell far below the highest figures for Paraguay.

Had López chosen to remain strictly on the defensive, he could have bade defiance to his enemies almost indefinitely. But this did not comport with his plans for the expansion of Paraguay and for the maintenance of what he rather pretentiously called "the equilibrium of La Plata." Accordingly, when the *Blanco* leader, Aguirre, called upon him to attack the Brazilian forces from the rear and thus force them to raise the siege of Montevideo, he complied with alacrity. But one serious obstacle stood in the way of the realization of this project. The Argentine territory of Missiones and the provinces of Corrientes and Entre Ríos lay between Paraguay and its two enemies. To come to the aid of the hard pressed *Blancos* it was necessary then to cross Argentine territory. Permission was asked of President Mitre and was naturally refused. It was then that López committed what was probably the greatest blunder of his career. Disregarding Mitre's prohibition, the Paraguayan dictator threw his troops into Corrientes, flagrantly violating the neutrality of Argentina. As was to be expected, President Mitre promptly declared war. Thus López found himself engaged in hostilities with the two foremost nations of South America. In defying the Argentine government he had counted on Urquiza's promised coöperation. But things fell out differently. By February, the Colorado chieftain, Flores, thanks to the support of the Brazilian army, was the recognized head of the Uruguayan government. To Paraguay's two enemies was now added a third. On May 1, 1865, was signed by Brazil, Uruguay, and Argentina the Treaty of Triple Alliance, by which the Allies, as we may henceforth call them, agreed not to lay down their arms until the power of López had been destroyed. . . .

9

Harris Gaylord Warren

The Paraguayan Image of the War of the Triple Alliance

Every war has at least two sides. The Paraguayan attitude on the war of 1865–1870 has been ably captured by Professor Harris Gaylord Warren of Miami University, author of books and articles on Paraguayan as well as Mexican history. It is clear from his account that Francisco Solano López was not without virtue and that Brazil was not without blame.

. . . Many students of Latin American history, including the present writer, have been too hasty in accepting the anti-López image of the war. We need to pay much more attention to what López and his writers insisted were Paraguayan motives in precipitating South America's most terrible war.

From Harris Gaylord Warren, "The Paraguayan Image of the War of the Triple Alliance," *The Americas,* XIX (July 1962), 3–10, 12–15, 17–20. Reprinted by permission of the publisher and the author.

The pro-López image of the war was constructed by the Marshal himself, a fact which may well make it suspect —but no more so than the image created by the Marshal's enemies. The central idea, the major thesis, is that the War of the Triple Alliance resulted from an attempt to destroy political equilibrium in the Plata basin. Brazil was the principal enemy of Platine equilibrium and Bartolomé Mitre committed a serious blunder in promoting civil war in Uruguay and then in joining with Brazil against Paraguay. Closely connected with this equilibrium argument is the thesis that Paraguay was fighting a war for survival. *Porteños* still dreamed of bringing the old viceregal area under their control, and Brazil's territorial appetite was insatiable. There is no room in this image of the war for a power-mad dictator of a militaristic nation who dreamed of making himself an emperor. The equilibrium-survival thesis requires a statesman of great foresight who led his people unwaveringly to their destiny. . . .

By political equilibrium, Paraguayans meant something more than a simple balance of power. Political equilibrium meant self-determination and also denied the right of intervention. Thus, neither Brazil nor Argentina could intervene in Uruguay without violating this concept. . . . It meant the right of nations to work out their own destinies. López believed that the peace and the liberty of the Plata area were "based on an equilibrium of forces between Brazil and Argentina, and the maintenance of that equilibrium was the basic objective and the key to every Paraguayan policy."

The roots of the Paraguayan War run deeply in South American history, and of this Paraguayans are well aware. But for this analysis of the contemporary Paraguayan image of the war, we need review only the critical years from 1859 to 1864. . . . During these years Paraguayans —and particularly López—formulated the equilibrium-survival thesis. López, indeed, used the word *equilibrio* so often that jeering Argentine papers called him *"el equi-librista."*

. . . Paraguayan relations with Brazil were far from happy in the 1850s. When Carlos Antonio López in 1853 refused to accept the Apá as Paraguay's northern boundary, the Brazilian chargé, Felipe José Pereira Leal, attempted to stir up a rebellion against him. López sent the foolish diplomat packing, and Brazil made warlike gestures that included troop concentrations and a naval expedition up the river. But López out-maneuvered or out-bluffed the Brazilians and relations were restored in March, 1855. A new treaty was signed in the following year, promising free navigation of the rivers and a definitive treaty of limits in 1862. Paraguay began to raise an army, built an arsenal, and constructed fortifications. Brazil then sent José María da Silva Paranhos, Visconde de Rio Branco, to Asunción in 1858 to negotiate a settlement. Francisco Solano López believed that Paraguay must accord free navigation or fight. Not ready for war, Carlos Antonio López approved a treaty which still left the limits question pending.

There was no secret about Paraguayan fears of Brazil. "The power that President [C. A.] López most fears," Charles Ames Washburn reported, "is Brazil. That is a vast empire and Paraguay on the map looks like a parallelogram taken out of it." Brazil, building up military supplies and troops in Mato Grosso, had no intention of settling the boundary question on Paraguayan terms. The old dictator had "a bitter hatred of the Brazilians and a contempt of them as soldiers, and in speaking of them usually calls them *macacos.* . . ."

Francisco Solano López, when he followed his father as dictator in 1862, sought an understanding with Brazil and with Argentina. This was necessary if he was to play a major role in Platine politics and defend the principle of equilibrium, a principle adhered to as early as 1855. But Brazil refused his overtures and Bartolomé Mitre, by supporting the Flores invasion of Uruguay, so aroused Paraguayan fears that a genuine accommodation became impossible. . . .

Argentine and Brazilian intervention in Uruguay in 1863 and 1864 led López to develop his equilibrium concept to the point where it became an obsession. *Blancos* were in power in Uruguay when Mitre became president of Argentina. The Uruguayan Colorado, Venancio Flores, had fought with Mitre and the latter was not one to ignore his debt. When Flores and his few companions landed in Uruguay in April, 1863, Argentine authorities were conveniently ignorant of the event. Later they permitted recruits and supplies to reach Flores. Uruguay's president, Bernardo P. Berro, believed that both Buenos Aires and Brazil were promoting the Colorado rebellion.

López, only moderately well informed about events, was much alarmed. He condemned Mitre's course, refused to believe that Buenos Aires was without guilt, and feared foreign intervention in Uruguay. . . .

. . . Brazil, at first interested in preventing Argentina from gaining an advantage in violation of the 1828 settlement, soon became involved in a quarrel with the *Blancos* which put the Empire and Argentina on the same side. Anastasio C. Aguirre, who became president of Uruguay in March, 1864, faced Brazilian intervention as well as the Argentine-sponsored Flores revolt. . . .

Brazilian intervention in the Uruguayan chaos aroused more fears in Asunción than in Buenos Aires. With Mitre and the Emperor both seeking their overthrow, the *Blancos* had nowhere to turn except to Paraguay and to possible enemies of Mitre in the riparian provinces. Argentine writers view *Blanco* diplomacy as an astute effort to deceive López into believing that Brazil intended to absorb Uruguay, and that a Brazilian-Argentine agreement existed to absorb Paraguay as well.

López and his foreign minister, José Berges, were not

simpletons. Their interest in Platine affairs needed no promptings from Montevideo. Nearly every issue of *El Semanario* carried news and editorials about Uruguayan developments. . . . López, indeed, fully believed that Uruguayan independence was indispensable for equilibrium in the Plata area and Paraguay's own survival. . . . Paraguayan alarm increased as evidence of Argentine and Brazilian aid to Flores increased. . . .

The climax in this concern over equilibrium came at the end of August [1864] in a Paraguayan warning to Brazil. López informed Brazil that Paraguay would "consider any occupation of the Oriental territory as threatening its integrity and sovereignty, a condition of equilibrium that it upholds as a principle of vital interest to Paraguay, and that for this reason it will not consent to any temporary or permanent occupation by Brazilian forces in the Oriental State of the Uruguay." Brazil clearly intended to make war, *El Semanario* editorialized, and rejected Paraguay's offer of mediation. "The principle of equilibrium of the States of the Plata involves the life, peace, and prosperity of the Republic. . . ." Brazilian occupation of Uruguay would be a "threat to the liberty, independence, sovereignty and territorial integrity of the Republic of Paraguay, and the other states of this part of America."

. . . Another editorial elaborated the ideological basis for the equilibrium, or balance of power, thesis:

> The system of politics proceeds from the supposition that force or power does not constitute right, that the weak have as much right as the strong to enjoy independence and sovereignty [and may combine forces to protect themselves]. The same motives that animate the Paraguayan people to assume the attitude that it has taken in regard to the pretensions of the Brazilian Empire in the Banda Oriental, that is to say, the motives of humanity, of justice, and of their

own security and preservation, should also animate the other states of the Plata, since each one, considering its past as well as its present circumstances, is interested in the maintenance of the equilibrium.

Two corollaries to the equilibrium-survival thesis are that Brazil was the principal enemy, and Argentina was committing a serious error in not supporting Paraguay. . . . Although Argentina's support of Flores could not have been far from his thoughts, López certainly did not take his eyes from Brazil. He was arming against eventualities; both Argentina and Brazil aroused his fears, but it was Brazil that he feared most.

Paraguayan fear of Brazil is easy to understand. Unsolved boundary disputes, arguments over navigation of the Paraguay, the expedition of 1856, and finally, intervention in Uruguay were sufficient cause for apprehension. Moreover, Brazilians were accumulating large stores of munitions at Coimbrá and Corumbá, perhaps to use in reducing Humaitá. . . .

. . . Paraguayans, and foreigners, too, felt that if Paraguay hadn't started the war, Brazil would have done so to its own advantage. Before the war really made much headway, Edward Thornton sought to have Mitre arbitrate the conflict. José María da Silva Paranhos desperately and successfully worked against this plan. He wanted the war to go on and promoted the Triple Alliance. . . . In the conference of Yataity-Corá on September 12, 1866, López suggested honorable terms for peace. Mitre and the Marquês de Caxias both urged acceptance, but Pedro II refused. Argentine participation in the war declined noticeably after the internal disturbances of late 1866, and an American minister, John L. Stevens, truthfully observed that "the chief actors in this sanguinary and criminal destruction were López and Brazil." . . .

. . . Paraguayans believed that this was a war for survival, and López emphasized this idea as a part of the equilibrium thesis. López believed that the fate of Paraguay and Uruguay were indissolubly linked, and that a plot existed between Brazil and Buenos Aires to absorb the two republics.

A basis for this charge was the understanding reached between Mitre and Brazil in May, 1864, an understanding formalized by the treaty of May 1, 1865. Mitre did not want to be genuinely neutral in the conflict. Paraguayan suspicions were of long standing. José Berges had suspected an Argentine-Brazilian alliance in May, 1863, and *Blanco* diplomacy played upon the suspicions that Paraguay's two rivals might combine to divide its territory. . . .

Fear of Argentine and Brazilian designs on Paraguayan territory may have been groundless before the war began. But any doubt vanished with the publication of the treaty of May 1, 1865.[1] The Allies wanted to keep the treaty secret. Its publication, thanks to the British government, caused widespread condemnation of the Allies among neutrals and aroused the determination of Paraguayans to resist to the end. . . .

The war was in a very real sense a bloody monument to ignorance and misunderstanding. Mitre, Sarmiento, and Elizalde apparently could not understand the deep and genuine concern felt in Asunción over developments in Platine politics. They should have understood how López and Berges thought. . . . It is indeed amazing that Mitre and Elizalde could not project to Asunción their own concern over Brazilian intentions in Uruguay.

López, too, was guilty of misunderstanding based in part on ignorance. He was convinced that an alliance existed

---

[1] In Article VIII the Allies pledged themselves "to respect the independence, sovereignty and territorial integrity of the Republic of Paraguay." Then in Article XVI, Brazil and Argentina are given all the territory in dispute, plus the Chaco Boreal to which Argentina had no good claim.

between Buenos Aires and Brazil long before May, 1865. This could be an alliance for the dismemberment of Paraguay. Having been unable to settle their boundary disputes to Paraguay's major disadvantage, Asunción's two traditional enemies might have decided to co-operate in eliminating Paraguay as a national unit. The [internationally guaranteed] settlement of 1828 and mutual suspicions could keep Buenos Aires and the Empire from absorbing all of Uruguay; but there were no such considerations protecting Paraguay. It was, therefore, perfectly natural that López should evolve his equilibrium-survival thesis.

López was concerned with equilibrium, and in being so concerned he was more than a step or two ahead of the great Mitre whose political acumen has been highly praised. For López was asking that sovereign states be treated as equals in the family of nations; he was seeking recognition of the principle that neighbors, even once removed, are mutually involved internationally. His world may have been somewhat less than the planet, but his world was one world.

❧10❧

Pelham Horton Box

━━━◆◀◉▶◆━━━

The Paraguayan War:
Reactionary Dictatorship
v Argentine Liberalism

*While attempting a balanced view, Dr. Pelham
Horton Box (1898–1937) nevertheless saw history
as a struggle between good and evil, and Paraguay
was more easily identified with the latter than the
former. But Argentina, not Brazil, is given the credit
for being the chief target of the Paraguayan dictator
Francisco Solano López.*

*The author, an Englishman, died prematurely
ten years after completing the doctoral thesis at the
University of Illinois from which this excerpt is taken.*

. . . The personality and ideas of this extraordinary man
[López] present immense problems to the investigator. Born
to power and enjoying the privileges of a Crown Prince
from boyhood, he had succeeded his father as President of
Paraguay in 1862 by a sort of disguised hereditary right.
He was the heir of the immense powers and political tradi-

From Pelham Horton Box, *The Origins of the Paraguayan War*
(Urbana: University of Illinois Press, 1930), pp. 280–284. Reprinted by permission of the publisher.

tions of the semi-plebiscitary dictatorship founded by Dr.
Francia and consolidated by his father, Carlos Antonio
López. A man of enormous will, boundless pride and intense, one might say Japanese, patriotism, he had been
accustomed to the machinery of administration and the
conduct of affairs from his earliest 'teens. He returned from
his two years of travel in Europe in 1853 and 1854 a
fervent admirer of Napoleon III and of the militaristic
despotism which the man of December had founded on the
will of the petty Bourgeoisie and the Napoleonic legend.
He had all his father's contempt for the "anarchists" of
Buenos Aires.

"What do you mean by liberty?" he asked Hector Varela.
"The kind you have in Buenos Aires? The liberty to insult
each other in the press, to kill each other in the district
assemblies for the election of Deputies, to keep the nation divided, for everyone to do what he fancies without
respect for anyone else?"

He thoroughly approved the economic paternalism represented by the monopoly of yerba, which the Paraguayan
Government jealously maintained in the teeth of bitter
attacks in those doctrinaire Liberal papers of Buenos Aires
which well reflected the opinions of baffled potential ex-
ploiters.

He inherited from his two predecessors a profound dis-
trust for the principles and designs of the *Porteños,* against
whom Paraguay had vindicated her right to independence
and from whose propaganda of "demagogy" Dr. Francia
had defended his people by the drastic means of absolute
isolation. . . . Opposition within Paraguay was out of the
question. An immense and efficient system of espionage
made all combination among the independent educated
class impossible. The only newspaper in Paraguay was
edited by the government. Practically every aspect of private life came under some form of state regulation (one
could not marry without the previous permission of the

government), but there is no evidence that the masses of the population resented this paternalism or felt it oppressive. . . .

Inevitably the philosophic liberalism of the Argentine Unitarian-Liberals was regarded by the López dynasty as a dangerous infection, from which Paraguay must be preserved at all costs. The Porteños returned the compliment by proclaiming the state that was the first to build a railway in this region of South America as a barbarous *terra incognita* peopled by hyperborean savages. The great achievements of the Paraguayan Government under Francia and Carlos Antonio López in maintaining internal order and external peace; in fostering agriculture and economic development; in organizing even a sketchy educational system, while Argentina, Uruguay, for a time Brazil and most of the other states were convulsed by desperate civil wars and weltered in what appeared to be a condition of endemic civil war have but rarely been justly appraised, for their memorials have vanished like the Jesuit Arcadia. . . .

Yet nineteenth century liberalism was to bear other fruit than anarchy in Latin America. Under Mitre it was to become the inspiration of a national reorganization and the refounding of Argentina. But between the Liberals of Buenos Aires and the strange and formidable Government of Paraguay there could in the end be no genuine appeasement; there was a fundamental conflict of principles. More and more the reactionaries of the Río de la Plata came to look upon Paraguay as the last stronghold against the Liberal revolution.

Though Dr. Francia's relations with Brazil had been generally friendly and though the Empire supported Carlos Antonio López against Rosas, after the battle of Caseros [1852] the relations of Paraguay and Brazil grew steadily worse. The long controversy between the two countries over the Blanco and Apa frontiers embittered Paraguayan feelings and convinced the suspicious President that Brazil was bent on absorbing his country. The Empire was certainly trying to win as much territory on the Rio Paraguay as possible in terms of the never-ending struggle for the all-important river-line. Carlos Antonio López refused to make the sacrifices necessary to come to a final settlement of all outstanding differences with either one of his two neighbors; at the same time he refrained from taking a forward policy, adhering to the tradition of Francia's aloofness. The logic of his attitude demanded extensive military preparations if Paraguay was to vindicate her rights against a possible combination of Buenos Aires and Brazil. These, largely under the insistent pressure of his son, he began.

Francisco Solano López was willing to draw the deduction from which his father shrank and envisage an aggressive war against both Brazil and Argentina, or rather that part of Argentina under the influence of the liberalism of Buenos Aires and exemplified in the leadership of Alsina and Mitre. If we are to believe Hector Varela, he had resolved on such a war as early as 1855.

Both members of the López dynasty expressed a great contempt for the Brazilian *macacos*. It has been a characteristic of the Spanish-Americans to underestimate the courage and abilities of the Portuguese.

Argentina throughout the '50s was in a state of chronic disorder and division which continued beyond [the battle of] Pavón [1861]. López II did not believe that Argentina could be reorganized under the leadership of Buenos Aires, but Pavón was an added reason for a forward policy. From the point of view of López the "pavonization" of Argentina spelt a dangerous triumph of those "demagogic" and "anarchic" principles which would disrupt his power if they ever took root in Paraguay.

His hostility to Buenos Aires and Brazil has two aspects. Under one he stands forth as the champion of Spanish America against the political and economic advance of the Empire towards the Río de la Plata. Under the other aspect he stands forth as the head of the international reaction within the Spanish-American world against the advance of the "demagogic" principles of the Argentine Liberals. Hence, his co-operation with the *Blancos* was natural enough. They were the Uruguayan party who had called in Rosas against their political enemies. By doing so they identified themselves with the despotism of their great ally. By defending Montevideo against Rosas and the Blancos the Colorados identified themselves with the cause of the Liberal enemies of the Dictator. The Blancos, though theoretically constitutional, became more and more conservative and reactionary. Herrera's dispatches are full of references to "the principle of authority." Berro and Aguirre constantly invoked this fatal formula, invariably used by reactionaries in opposing any kind of reform. Who could represent "the principle of authority" better than Francisco Solano López? So, we have seen the adumbrations of an alliance of López, the reactionary provinces of Argentina and the Blancos in Uruguay against revolutionary Buenos Aires and imperialist Brazil. Clearly we have here the rough sketch of an imperial policy involving the reorganization of Argentina on a reactionary basis; the foreshadowing of a new confederation of which the Sparta of South America, Paraguay, would be the heart: reactionary, despotic, militaristic.

The idea has a certain grandeur, nor did it lack feasibility. But its execution required abilities of the highest order. It was not enough to have a reliable army and unprepared enemies. Foresight and statesmanship were required, and in both López failed lamentably. . . .

II

The First Republic

W. T. Stead

◄◆►

The Eagle of The Hague

*In 1889 the Empire was overthrown by army of-
ficers who had risen to prominence during and after
the Paraguayan War. The coup d'état and the subsequent years of military rule discredited Brazil
abroad. After 1894 the civilian-run government devoted much of its effort toward restoring the image
of Brazil as a stable and "civilized" country.*

*The success of this effort may be measured by the
following article by W. T. Stead, a prominent British
newspaperman who covered the Second Hague
Peace Conference in 1907. It is not surprising that
Rui Barbosa (1849–1923)—liberal, cultured, for-
eign-oriented—was chosen to represent his country
at this congress. His consuming belief in the rights of
the individual was now translated into a ringing defense of the rights of each sovereign nation. And he
here displayed the same intransigent, uncompromising, and self-defeating righteousness that led to his
failure in so many other good causes.*

Brazil has this year made her *début* on the world-stage,
and the *débutante* has acquitted herself with such brilliant
success that the event demands universal attention.

From W. T. Stead, "Brazil at The Hague," *The Review of Reviews*,
XXXVI, No. 215 (November 1907), Supplement, 2–6, 11–13.

The place selected as the stage for this first appearance
was The Hague. . . . How did she acquit herself? That is
the story which I, who was a spectator in the front seats,
am now going to tell, deeming it a matter of no small historical interest and one which for the honor and glory of
Brazil should be placed on record. . . .

The first hint that the Conference received as to the
importance of the South Americans was the appointment,
at the suggestion of Russia, of Dr. [Rui] Barbosa as Président d'Honneur of the First Commission. The post of the
Président d'Honneur is solely honorary. It is a mark attest-
ing the distinction of the delegates. . . .

When the nominations were published and people began to ask who was this Dr. Barbosa, who at his very first
appearance was selected for so high an honor, the answer
given by the Russians was that Dr. Barbosa was one of the
most distinguished men in the Conference; he was an Ambassador, he was Vice-President of the Brazilian Senate,
and that he was reputed to be one of the greatest orators
and one of the most learned jurists in South America.
Curiosity being whetted rather than appeased by this description, further inquiries elicited the fact that Dr. Barbosa, although only fifty-six years of age, had had a long,
distinguished career. From a youth he had been both a student and a man of action. Deputy under the Empire, having
refused in 1889 the post of Minister of the Interior in the
last cabinet of the monarchy, he had taken an active part
in the revolution which terminated the monarchy of the
New World. He has been journalist, jurist, legislator, and
leader of the Opposition. When the Empire fell he was
the man entrusted with the task of forming the new Constitution for Brazil. It also fell to his lot to arrange for the
separation of Church and State in the new Republic—a
task which in every other country has been fatal to many
a reputation, but which in Brazil was accomplished with no
breach of the friendly relations which existed between the
two high contracting parties.

When the Brazilian Navy revolted Dr. Barbosa had to flee from the country for a season, and like many other distinguished refugees he found London a pleasant place of exile. England has ever been to him a second Fatherland. He excited considerable indignation in Brazil on one occasion by declaring that if the choice had been given him where to be born he would probably have selected England as his birthplace. During the two years he remained in London he wrote a series of "letters from England," which have deservedly earned a popular reputation in Brazil, where they are regarded as affording the best account as to the social and political ideas in England during the last ten years of the nineteenth century. But all these other marks of distinction were overshadowed by the discovery of the fact that Dr. Barbosa, first of all living men, had discovered the injustice of the treatment of Captain Dreyfus, and had publicly condemned his sentence before anyone else had protested against it. This fact, recently attested by Captain Dreyfus, gave Dr. Barbosa a cachet of distinction.

Dr. Barbosa had returned to Brazil after his exile, where he at once resumed a position among the leading statesmen of the Republic. Had his ambition lain in that direction he might have been elected President, and rumor said that whether he liked it or not he would probably be selected as President [Afonso] Pena's successor [in 1910]. It was believed, however, that he preferred to study in his library rather than to compete for political honors. His collection of books is the best private library in South America, and one of the best in the world. He has not given up the practice of law, and, having received from the Senate in Brazil the task of finishing the work of her Civil Code begun in the Chamber of Deputies, he will, when he goes back to his own country, return to the practice of his profession, in which his reputation as jurist is second to none in South America.

Such were the things that men heard about Dr. Barbosa; but the members of the Conference were not left long in doubt as to the quality and caliber of the Member for Brazil. From the first sittings of the Conference Dr. Barbosa took part in all the more important debates with quiet composure and imperturbable demeanor which caused him first to be a butt of ridicule, and then of resentment. But ridicule and resentment both soon gave place to a feeling of respect, not unmixed with a certain element of awe. Dr. Barbosa was felt to be a first-class fighting man, who was never more effective than when he was attacking. He gave more than one of his assailants a taste of his quality which caused them to leave him severely alone for the future.

It is difficult to imagine a greater contrast than that between the general estimate of Dr. Barbosa in the first and in the last week of the Conference. In the first week everyone voted him a bore of gigantic dimensions; he was nicknamed "Verbosa." The apparition of this quiet little stranger who had got something to say, and was determined to say it in his own way and in his own time, irritated many of his fellow-members, who endeavored to drown his voice by the simple expedient of entering into conversation with their nearest neighbors. When Dr. Barbosa was on his legs at one of the earlier sittings, a delegate reported that Dr. Barbosa began to speak at four o'clock, and at first his was the only voice in the hall, but the last half-hour of his speech his was only the voice among two hundred which were all going at the same time.

The Conference, it was said, "could never stand Barbosa." But the Conference soon learned to "stand Barbosa," and it was not very long in recognizing the fact that he was one of the most powerful men in the Assembly. The two greatest personal forces in the Conference were Baron [Adolf] Marschall [von Bieberstein] of Germany and Dr. Barbosa of Brazil. Behind Baron Marschall was the whole armed might of the German Empire, which was close at hand, and constantly present before the eyes of all the delegates. Behind Dr. Barbosa there was an unknown distant

Republic, incapable of taking any military action, and with a fleet which had not yet left the stocks. Nevertheless, of the two men Dr. Barbosa counted for more than Baron Marschall when the Conference ended. A greater personal triumph no member achieved at the late Conference, and it was the more remarkable because it was achieved single-handed without any outside aid. Dr. Barbosa had no allies; he had many rivals and many enemies, but he had come out on top. It was an immense personal triumph, which redounded enormously to the credit of Brazil. . . .

The issue which was then presented to the Conference was one of those great problems in politics which from time to time arise to probe the heart and challenge the judgment of mankind. It is seldom that a political issue so vital has been brought forward so suddenly, in such clearly-cut shape, so free from all confusing side issues. The question thus raised will not be settled in a year, possibly not even in a generation, for it goes right down to the roots of things, and appeals to the most strongly opposing principles which govern human action. That question in its essence was whether Might or Right should be the dominant factor in the affairs of man. Granting that Might, expressed in armed force, dominated the world, ought it therefore to follow as a necessary corollary that Might should also be enthroned on the judgment seat which had to interpret international law in accordance with sound principles of justice and equity? It is a question upon which all men can honestly differ.

The Conference was fortunate in having the opposing sides of this controversy advocated by men capable of rising to the height of this great argument. Baron Marschall, representative of Germany, stood firmly defiant as an advocate of Might, Dr. Barbosa, at the same time stepping forth unhesitatingly as David before Goliath of Gath, stood up to advocate the cause of Right. The two antagonists

were not unevenly matched, except for their strongly contrasting physical bulk. Baron Marschall was the tallest man
in the Conference with the doubtful exception of M. [José
Battle y] Ordoñez, ex-President of Uruguay; Dr. Barbosa
was the most diminutive delegate in the Ridderzaal. Both
were jurists, both were orators, both were old parliamentari-
ans, and both were absolutely imbued with the conviction
that they were right, and that their opponent was utterly
and demonstrably mistaken. It was by the way that he
conducted his side of this great controversy that Dr.
Barbosa rallied behind him Latin America, and succeeded
ultimately in detaching North Americans from their German ally.

The argument on either side was well sustained with
much vehement eloquence and forceful logic. Baron
Marschall took his stand upon the right divine of Might
to be supreme even upon the judgment-seat. "I have a
great respect for Might," he said, "and what it represents
in the world. Never will I consent to allow a great incarna-
tion of might like the German Empire to be tried by a
judge representing Guatemala." On the other hand, Dr.
Barbosa maintained that the equal sovereign right of every
independent State lay at the very foundations of juris-
prudence, and that to constitute a Court in which every
sovereign State had not an equal right to sit on the
judgment-seat was to outrage every principle of international law. At first the United States supported the German
view, and in a series of outlines sketched out a scheme
by which the German principle should be put into practical
effect. There were many drafts—suggestions rather than
proposals; but all embodied the fundamental principle of
the inequality of the Powers in the Constitutional Court.
Assuming that there was to be a Court of seventeen judges,
it was demanded that one-half of the Court at least should
be confined exclusively to the representatives of the great
Powers. The definition of the great Powers varied. At one

time it included Holland and Turkey; another time Spain was added out of deference to its past glories, a plea which might equally have justified the inclusion of Greece. In the first suggestion China figured as one of the great Powers of the world, entitled to a great Power's rank upon the judgment-seat on account of its population, which includes one-fourth of the human race; afterwards, when it was pointed out that no European Power would allow a Chinese police magistrate to sit in judgment on a drunken European sailor, China was summarily degraded from her position as a first-rate Power and relegated to second or third rank. But these various changes excited animosity without disarming opposition, for none of them affected the fundamental principle, which was, that a certain number of Powers, whether it was eight or whether it was eleven, ought to be singled out from the forty-four sovereign and independent States represented at the Conference, and accorded a position paramount in the proposed Court of Arbitral Justice. They were to have their judges sitting on the Bench all the time; the remaining thirty or thirty-six Powers were to be allowed to nominate the minority of the judges to take their places upon the Bench in turn.

The immediate result of the production of this project was to create a revolt among the smaller Powers, and especially among the Latin Americans. The Foreign Minister of Brazil seems to have sent round the fiery cross from Rio to all the South American capitals, emphasizing the outrage which this proposal inflicted upon the principle of the equal rights of all sovereign States. As a net result delegation after delegation received explicit instructions to support Dr. Barbosa, who from the first took his stand unhesitatingly against every proposal which did not secure every Power an equal opportunity of sitting as judge on the Supreme Court of Arbitral Justice which the Conference was asked to establish. For a brief period there was a feeling of sharp and almost bitter antagonism between

Dr. Barbosa and the North American Delegation. But after duly surveying the ground the North American Delegation came to the conclusion that it was absolutely impossible to establish a Court excepting on the basis of equal rights for all sovereign States. They accordingly dropped all their previous projects, and brought forward as their final suggestion a proposal that the judges should be elected by all the Powers; every Power having fifteen votes to distribute them among fifteen candidates of their own nomination, and the fifteen who received most votes to be constituted the Court. This conceded the principle of the equal right of every sovereign independent State. But it did not satisfy Dr. Barbosa, neither did it please Baron Marschall; and both Dr. Barbosa and Baron Marschall voted against the American proposal. That vote was fatal. After it was registered all that remained to be done was to substitute for the *projet* a pious *voeu* expressing the hope that the Powers would establish the Court after they had arrived at an agreement as to the method for appointing the judges.

The controversy has not ended, it has only been begun. Dr. Barbosa succeeded in destroying every proposition which in his judgment was inconsistent with the sovereign right of each independent State. Baron Marschall, who also had assisted in destroying the American project after it had been amended in order to meet the views of Dr. Barbosa, may be credited with a share in the victory, but it was a victory achieved by the sacrifice of an object to which he had declared he attached supreme importance. Dr. Barbosa never wished to have any other Court than that which at present exists. Baron Marschall, on the contrary, had declared himself as an advocate of the new Permanent Court. If he succeeded in one object he failed in the other. Dr. Barbosa succeeded in both.

F. J. de Oliveira Vianna

Ideal and Real: Constitutional Provisions and Political Practice

Neither the abolition of slavery nor the declaration of the republic had brought about the sought-after solution to Brazil's problems, and it was not long before disillusionment set in. The sociologist and pensador Francisco José de Oliveira Vianna (1885–1951) sought another explanation for Brazil's backwardness than those proposed by abolitionists and republicans. In some of his work he finds this explanation in race—he was, after all, a man of his time. But in the present selection he speaks more broadly of the milieu—and he verges on being ahead of his time. For he finds, as do many reformers today, that the inequality of power within a latifundiary system is at least partly to blame for his country's condition. On the other hand, he calls for a political system that is "adapted to our people," thus foreshadowing the thought of the dictator Getúlio Vargas

Translated from F. J. de Oliveira Vianna, "O idealismo da constituição," in A. Carneiro Leão, *et al., Á margem da historia da republica (ideaes, crenças e affirmações)* (Rio de Janeiro: Annuario do Brasil, 1924), pp. 138–140, 142–144, 146, 157–160.

*and of the present authoritarian government on the
need for so-called realistic political forms. It is also
curious how Oliveira Vianna here plays upon that
leitmotif of Brazilian political writers: the proliferat-
ing, unproductive bureaucracy. Ahead of his time
or not, Oliveira Vianna was widely read and widely
quoted and his pessimism became characteristic of
the First Republic.*

The republican faction at the time of the 1889 coup d'état
was really a relatively insignificant minority spread throughout the country, with its centers of greatest activity in Rio
de Janeiro and São Paulo. The bulk of the electorate was
made up of the two traditional factions: the Liberals and
the Conservatives. When a republic was created, these old
partisan groups disappeared, breaking up into thousands of
little fragments, each one consisting of a small clan grouped
about a minor leader. As a rule, this small-time political
boss did not represent—at least not in the provinces—the
most prestigious local political elements: the most prestigious and refined members of the old local aristocracy either
withdrew at the time of the coup d'état, closeting themselves
within the platonic cult of the monarchy, or took up a discreet attitude awaiting the ultimate course of events. Thus,
the majority of the partisan clans, which organized themselves throughout the country in substitution for the old
monarchical organizations, did not have the most authoritative figures from the old elite at their forefront. There were
instead—with notable and brilliant exceptions—many inter-
lopers, climbers, political nouveaux riches, without solidity
of character and without scruples to ballast their con-
sciences. They rushed headlong into the positions abandoned by the old guard with the indiscipline and incon-
sistency of raiding bandits sacking a deserted city. . . .

For many people the republic was a last-moment inspiration; for others, a simple movement of revenge; and for still others—*republicanos históricos,* for example—merely a theme for sonorous speeches and never a clear, profound conviction "written on the fleshy tablets of the heart." Thus, when the old regime fell, republican thought had not yet attained its full maturity; it had not yet saturated the consciousness of the country. Therefore, the exponents of the republican ideal—in the Constituent Assembly or outside of it—did not seem to be masters of their main idea. The impression they leave us is that they did not really know what they wanted or what had to be done. Good boys at heart, they were adept at throwing rocks at the government and were now caught by surprise in the grave mission of being statesmen; they hurriedly had to improvise a constructive program. Preoccupied since 1870 with merely opposing the government (as we Brazilians are accustomed to doing), they had not really thought about it before November 14, 1889; and when on the 16th they were forced to think of it, they were visibly embarrassed.

Until then they had contented themselves with a vague program of vague aspirations formulated in vague phrases: "immortal principles," the "weight of opinion," the "sovereignty of the people," "federal organization," the "principle of liberty," "democracy," the "republic," and so on. The Manifesto of 1870 is a magnificent example of this cult of reverberating generalities that made up the whole mentality of those who campaigned in behalf of republican ideas. When, twenty years later, they took possession of the government of the country, this literary, oratorical, and doctrinaire pattern had not been modified one iota.

The most distinctive trait of this mentality was the belief in the power of written formulas. For these dreamers, to laboriously write down an idea was, in and of itself, to make it a reality. To put a constitution on paper was immediately to make it a living and vibrant thing: words had the magic power of giving life and blood to the ideas that they represented. . . .

Now, these ideas lacked a social class to give them flesh and blood. The realization of a great ideal is never the collective work of the mass, but of an elite, a group, a class that identifies itself with that ideal, that fights for it, and that, when victorious, gives it reality and assures its execution. Now, the republican constitution, synthesis of the aspirations of the evangelists of the new regime, lacked all this. The republican clique, as we have already seen, was really very small and represented neither a closely knit core nor a prestigious social class. It was made up of scattered elements coming from all classes and was, after all, nothing more than a tiny band of dreamers flitting about in fitful and unfocused activity within an apathetic, indifferent, and immense country. Therefore, the politicians who were responsible for putting into action the new and delicate institutional mechanisms were, in the majority (particularly in the states), entirely alien to the idealism of the republican evangelists. And thus, when they acted, they did so not as men of belief transfigured by the Faith, but merely as men of their time, of their milieu, and of their race—which is equivalent to saying, as we shall see, that they acted in complete contradiction to the idealistic spirit of the constitution.

Furthermore, the economic conditions of the society were completely unsuited to the rise of political idealism. The abolition of slave labor [1888] exploded with the violence of a subterranean mine; and the entire society from top to bottom staggered, shook, and, at many points collapsed entirely. The structure of all classes was profoundly altered—some directly, such as the agricultural class; others indirectly as a repercussion of the blow upon the planters.

It was within this agitated and unstable medium that the republic arose and the new constitution was promulgated.

The abolition of slave labor had disrupted the means of livelihood for the aristocracy; and when the republic was declared, this group was urgently seeking a new economic base. Now, this situation was evidently the least suitable for the survival of an unselfish and disinterested spirit so indispensable for the implementation of the high, idealistic principles expressed in the text of the constitution. Even worse, this aristocracy, dislodged from its great properties, sought a new source of funds in the state. This new basis of wealth was the industry of public employment, which the new regime founded and which became for the aristocracy more advantageous and lucrative than the old and now profoundly disorganized industry of exploiting the land. In fact, the new regime, because of its democratic character and because of its decentralizing and federative spirit, prodigiously multiplied administrative and legislative positions in the union, the states, and the counties. So the political elite, mainly composed of the very people who had been "uprooted" by abolition, quickly oriented itself toward elective and administrative functions and made of public employment the axis of all their aspirations. In these conditions, public posts, whether administrative or political, came to be contested not as the most efficient means for realizing the "ideal," the "dream," but purely and effectively as a means for gaining a livelihood. . . .

Those who were successful in perching in this way on these official or elective posts logically saw in them definitive and lifelong positions; and they defended their posts against the assaults of new invaders by all means available. The invaders, pressed by the same categorical imperative, fought for the positions of power with the aggressive roughness of one who overruns a trench. And for both groups all means were considered fair, from unrestrained fraud to manifest illegality and blatant plunder, from the fusillade of diatribes and printed calumny to the more powerful and booming cannonades of real armed force. . . .

Republican idealism, therefore, failed from the beginning of its constitutional experience because the circumstances of the historical moment that surrounded the first years of the new regime were completely hostile to the rise of any idealistic spirit. However, even if those circumstances had been favorable, the beautiful ideology of the Constituent Assembly would have failed in the same manner—if not immediately, as it did occur, at least with the passage of time—as the disagreement between its principles and the mental and structural conditions of our people became more obvious. . . .

Two typical attitudes were the result, two different opinions that divided the early republicans and even today continue to divide them: the "intolerant" attributed the failure of the system to the corruption of those who retained power, and the "tolerant" believed the bankruptcy of the system was merely outward appearance since it arose from the lack of "experience" or "understanding" of the new institutions. . . . Even today the descendants of the latter continue messianically to await the action of the great miracle maker.

But the former—those of the intolerant current—less forbearing and not the least fatalistic, place their faith not in time but in force, or, more properly in . . . violence. . . . They frequently appeal to the barracks, become quadrennial entrepreneurs of "salvation" in order to throw out of power the "corrupters of institutions," the "violators of the supreme law." When they are victorious they themselves attempt to give reality to the ideology of the constitution, but the fact is that until this day all these attempts of the party of force have been invariably crowned by failure. Until now no one has been successful in making concrete the "dream" of the dreamers of 1870 and 1891. . . .

The problem of our political reorganization is much more complex than appears to those who think they can resolve it with simple constitutional reforms. . . . The error of these theorizing souls, or, more correctly, their illusion, is the conviction, which they all share, that a *political* reform is only possible through *political means*. They do not understand that there may be other methods that can modify the conditions of political life in a society besides the modification of institutions created by public law.

Now in the Brazilian case, for example, political (that is, constitutional) reforms will merely be auxiliary to other greater reforms of a social and economic character that are needed to establish here a "democratic regime," "rule by opinion," "government of the people and by the people." One can even say that the establishment of this kind of political system in our country is first of all a social and economic problem and only secondarily a political and constitutional one.

One example will suffice to clarify this point. The bulk of our electorate, as we know, is outside the cities and consists of our rural population. Now nine-tenths of our rural population is composed, due to our economic organization and our civil legislation, of pariahs without land, without homes, without justice, and without rights; and all these people are entirely dependent on the great landowners. So that even if they were *conscious* of their political rights (which they are not) and wished to exercise them in an autonomous manner, they could not. And this is because the least desire for independence on the part of these pariahs would be punished by immediate expulsion and banishment by the landowners. The electoral mass, therefore, does not have *independence* of opinion.

Now, the most efficient means to secure that independence certainly will not be "universal suffrage," "direct election," "secret ballot," or "local self-government," but other means of an economic and social nature: the establishment of the "small holding"; a system of "long-term rental" or a "tenancy system in which the government would own the land"; the diffusion of the "corporate spirit" and "institutions of social solidarity"; an expeditious, prompt, and efficacious "juridical organization," and an "autonomous magistracy" with moral and material force to dominate the arbitrariness of the local bosses, and so on. None of these reforms are of a political or constitutional nature; but only they will be able to give to our rural populace—the basis of the national electorate—those indispensable attributes of independence and uprightness without which the famous "sovereignty of the people" has no meaning whatsoever.

This is only one of a thousand [possible] examples, but it is enough to demonstrate how the great modifications of our political life lie outside the exclusive dominion of purely constitutional reforms. Reforms of the text of our constitution will represent merely *one* of the means of our political reorganization and even then only an accessory or subsidiary one, never the principal one, and much less the *only* one.

This manner of facing the problem of our political reorganization is evidently antagonistic to the old idealism of the *históricos*. These were deductive souls who began with certain utopian postulates and from them extracted the structural elements of their political system. They lacked an objective sense of reality and did not think it necessary to possess it. Having to formulate a constitution for Brazil or for Cambodia, for the English or for a kraal of Hottentot land, they would create the same system of government with the same parts, the same connections, the same structure, the same way of operation, the same brakes, and the same safety valves. They would not modify anything in this machinery—not even the size of the head of a screw—because this would be equivalent to compromising the "beauty of the regime" or breaking the "harmony of the system."

Now, we cannot continue to cultivate this ingenuous condition of soulful constitutional aesthetes. Our objective will be neither "harmony" nor "beauty," but "compatibility" and "adaptation"; what we should seek are not beautiful or harmonious systems, but systems that are compatible with and adapted to our people.

ᵛᵍ13ᵉᵛ

Paulo Prado

The Roots of Brazilian Sadness

The disillusionment created by the First Republic is expressed in a book by Paulo Prado (1869–1943) subtitled An Essay on Brazilian Sadness. *The wealthy scion of a prominent coffee planter, Paulo Prado was both an active businessman and an introspective intellectual. The present work, first published in 1928, reflects the tensions produced by the encounter of an old-fashioned racism once endorsed by European science—and still prevalent among the intellectuals of the First Republic—and the eager acceptance of a more modern anthropology by a younger generation with which Prado was in close contact. His examination of Brazil's sexual-social history foreshadowed the work of the famous Brazilian writer Gilberto Freyre, although Prado, unlike Freyre, still suspected race mixture had cast an indelible stain upon his country.*

In a postscript to this book Prado called for a moralizing revolution that, as a substitute for war,

---

Translated from Paulo Prado, *Retrato do Brasil. Ensaio sôbre a tristeza brasileira,* 5th ed. (São Paulo: Editôra Brasiliense, 1944), pp. 11, 16, 29, 31, 33–34, 48, 60, 76–77, 102–103, 104–109. Printed by permission of the publisher.

would inject virility and strength into a decadent
society. The rise to power of Getúlio Vargas in 1930
and his subsequent adoption of a pseudofascist
language gave special relevance to Prado's Portrait
of Brazil. *But the more historical selections below*
have been chosen in an attempt to capture the
extreme pessimism that, despite his disclaimers,
dominates the book and made it highly controversial
in its day.

In a radiant land lives a sad people. It inherited this
melancholy from the discoverers who revealed this land to
the world and peopled it. The splendid dynamism of these
rough fellows was activated by two great drives that
dominated the psychology of the discovery and never produced happiness: love of gold and free and unbridled
sensuality. . . .

The culmination of their adventure was the encounter of
the European emerging from a temperate zone with the
exuberance of a natural setting characterized by strength
and grace. . . . Purely animal sexual unions were encouraged by the climate, man's freedom in a solitary vast-
ness, and the sensual Indian. The Edenic impression that
struck the imagination of newcomers was emphasized by
the naked charm of indigenous women. The very letter
written by [Vaz de] Caminha [in 1500] speaks of the
surprise of the sailors at the unexpectedly graceful figures
frolicking across the countryside. . . .

To the seductiveness of the land was allied the adolescent
dash of the adventurer. For men who came from a policed
Europe, the ardor of [native] temperaments, the amorality
of customs, the absence of civilized modesty, and all the
voluptuous swelling of virgin nature were an invitation to
a freewheeling and unrestrained life in which nothing was
forbidden. The Indian, in turn, was a lascivious animal,

living without any constraints upon the satisfaction of his carnal desire. . . .

The contact of dissolute and unruly conquistadors with this sensuality produced our first mixed-breed population. A land of all vices and all crimes. According to the testimony of contemporary Portuguese writers, the immorality of the first colonists was startling and went beyond all measure. . . . It was not moderated, but, rather, intensified by the infantile passivity of the African woman, who encouraged and developed the erotic heightened excitement in which the conquistador and the settler lived and which so deeply stamped their psychic make-up.

Another passion, however, dominated him. An even more tyrannical one: Greed. . . . The adventurer everywhere ran after silver, gold, and precious stones. For almost two centuries these were nothing more than dreams and fruitless illusions. But the sterility of this effort was compensated for by the capture of Indians. Slave hunting and prospecting expeditions were intertwined and intermingled. Whenever the mirage of rich mines evaporated, the enslaved Indian remained as consolation. . . .

The fascination with mines, however, had invaded all Brazil. It was a continuous obsession shared by all classes as a collective madness. This characteristic of our national formation is almost unique in the history of peoples. The ethnic conglomerations of the colony—the most varied from north to south—had no other ideal, no other incentive but this mean search in the bowels of mountains and among the gravel of distant streams and rivers. . . .

The dissolute life of Portugal was associated with misery and weakness, hidden by formulas of devout religiosity as poverty and debility were covered by apparent splendor and by a language of omnipotence. . . . Immorality reigned everywhere, especially among the clergy: the monasteries luxuriously supported concubines and children, maintained stables full of sleek and expensive horses, and kept purebred dogs and falcons. Society was made up of an intimate mixture of Moors and Negroes, some free, some slaves. Slave labor from Africa sustained agriculture; but bondage undermined the social organism, as it has done wherever it has existed. . . . So Brazil's settlement was begun by a people already infected by the leprous germ of decadence. . . .

Upon the first contact of the Portuguese with the physical and social surroundings of their exile, new and varied influences would take hold of them and transform them into a people neither like nor really different from those who left the motherland. Two tyrannical emotions dominated them: sensualism and love of gold. The history of Brazil is the disordered development of these obsessions that subjugated the body and soul of the victims.

As we have said, three factors contributed to exaggerated eroticism: the climate, the land, and the Indian woman or African slave girl. In the virgin land everything incited the cult of sexual vice. What we know of this embryonic society at the end of the century of discovery is a witness to the deliriums of erotic obsession. Indelible traces of these sensual excesses remained in the Brazilian character. The characteristics of exhaustion are found not only in the physical and sensorial qualities but also in the realm of intelligence and feeling. They produced somatic and psychic disturbances accompanied by profound fatigue that easily took on pathological qualities, from disgust to hatred.

On the other hand, as a consequence of this passion, another emotion rose up in the soul of the conqueror and settler, another debilitating emotion in its materialistic sterility: the exclusive fascination for gold, a virtual mania. . . .

A sad race was created by the struggle between these appetites—with no other ideal or goal, neither religious nor esthetic, with no political, intellectual, or artistic interest. The melancholy of venereal abuses and the melancholy of the single-minded pursuit of riches—the purposeless absorption in these insatiable passions—are deep scars on our racial psyche. . . . The exaltation of these instincts formed the special atmosphere in which the inhabitants of the colony lived and multiplied.

The development of a mournful tendency is doubtless a characteristic result among individuals and societies lessening in physical energy or weakening (if not completely lacking) in mental activity. The old medical adage asserts that *post coitum animal triste, nisi gallus qui cantat;* this condition is the "collapse" of which doctors speak—a physical and spiritual depression, continuous in those cases of repeated excesses. In Brazil sadness followed the intense sexual life of the colonist misled by erotic perversions of a decidedly atavistic quality.

And, in its turn, greed is a morbid creature, a sickness of the soul with symptoms, causes, and course. It can absorb all mental energy, with neither medicines to stop its development nor cure for its evils. Among us, for centuries, it was an unsatisfied passion, converted into an *idée fixe* by the very disillusion that followed it. It absorbed all the dynamic activity of the adventuresome colonist, without ever granting him the satiety of wealth or even the tranquillity of having reached a goal. The anxious and laborious search and the subsequent deception also produce a despondent feeling. Useless effort, aftertaste of disillusion. Lasciviousness, greed: melancholy. . . .

There are nations that are happy and there are nations that are sad. . . . Buckle would say that differences in climate explain the variations of temperament: countries of light and heat affect the psychology of the population; fog and darkness of rigorous winters lend a melancholy air to the men of cold lands. But in Brazil the veil of sadness stretches over the entire country in all its latitudes, despite the splendor of nature, from the mixed-breed woodsman of the Amazon basin and the parched deserts of the northeast to the gloomy and moody impassivity of the *paulista* or *mineiro*.

14

Robert J. Alexander

Brazilian *Tenentismo*

The sterility of the First Republic and the failure to deliver on the promise of change implied by its very establishment almost inevitably produced a reaction. Professor Robert J. Alexander of Rutgers University, well known for his interest in the history of social reform and labor organization in Latin America, here discusses the most important of these Brazilian protest movements. Young army lieutenants drawn from the emerging urban middle classes not only misunderstood the Brazilian peasant whom they vainly tried to stir up, but also failed to mobilize the political forces of the cities into a new reformist party.

In order to understand Tenentismo, one must comprehend the important role of the Brazilian army in the last half century. It was the military who ousted the last emperor and established the Republic; subsequently, the army took very seriously its role as the chief defender of the Republic and the supporter of constitutionalism. During the first

From Robert J. Alexander, "Brazilian 'Tenentismo,'" *Hispanic American Historical Review*, XXXVI (May 1956), 229–242. The following selection is from pp. 229–235. Reprinted by permission of the author and the publisher, Duke University Press.

thirty years after the founding of the Republic the army
intervened in politics numerous times, and various of its
leaders served as president.

The Republic and the army's participation in its affairs
did not change the facts of the economy and politics of
Brazil, which remained essentially a rural nation, dependent
almost completely on one or two crops—principally coffee
—for its foreign exchange and its prosperity. The political
power remained in the hands of the owners of the vast
coffee and sugar *fazendas*. The presidency tended to rotate
between the favorite sons of the large states of São Paulo
and Minas Geraes, none of whom desired or seriously
attempted to change the status quo.

However, the first World War brought certain changes.
Because the country was cut off from its principal sources
of supply for manufactured goods—particularly foodstuffs
and textiles—factory industry received a tremendous shot
in the arm. Manufacturing increased rapidly and with it
the middle class and the industrial working class gained
in numbers and importance. Both the new middle class and
the workers resented the continued domination of the
country by the landholding aristocracy. As occurred widely
throughout Latin America in the post-World War I period,
this discontent gave rise to new political developments.

Even before World War I a labor movement had been
born in Brazil. In 1909 the first central labor organization,
the Confederação Operaria Brasileira, was established under anarcho-syndicalist influence. During the war the labor
movement gained much ground, and there were several
important strikes, perhaps the most notable being a walkout
of 150,000 textile workers in Rio de Janeiro and other
cities in 1919. The governments of the time were not
sympathetic to the labor movement; even some years later
a leading political figure declared that "labor is a problem
for the police," a sentiment which was widely shared in
ruling circles.

However, labor and middle class unrest did meet with ι certain sympathetic response among the younger officers of the army, most of whom were drawn from the middle class and shared the discontent of these elements. The first evidence of this unrest in the army came to light in 1922, when the soldiers of the Copacabana fortress on the outskirts of Rio de Janeiro rose in revolt, led by their junior officers, of whom the principal leaders were Antonio Siqueira Campos and Eduardo Gomes. This revolt was fairly easily suppressed by loyal elements in the army.

In 1924 a much more serious revolt occurred in the city of São Paulo. It was led by Major Miguel Costa, Commander of São Paulo's state militia, supported by General Isidoro Dias Lopes, Joaquim and Juarez Távora, Eduardo Gomes, Cordeiro de Farias and João Alberto, all of whom were junior officers except General Dias Lopes. The rebels captured the city of São Paulo and held it for almost a month. As loyal troops gathered outside the city, the forces of Major Costa withdrew and started the long march towards the Iguassú River, in southwestern Brazil.

Meanwhile, the regular army's battalion of railroad engineers headed by twenty-six year old Captain Luís Carlos Prestes, had revolted in the southernmost state of Brazil, Rio Grande do Sul, in sympathy with the São Paulo rebels. After fighting their way through greatly superior government troops, the Costa and Prestes groups joined forces somewhere near the mighty Iguassú Falls. The united forces reorganized, with Major Costa as the nominal commander-in-chief and Luís Carlos Prestes as chief of general staff.

The fighting force, which at times dwindled to only a few hundred men, was the famous Prestes Column. It took this name from its second-in-command, who was the military genius of the Column, rather than from its commander-in-chief. In the succeeding three years, it wandered back and forth across Brazil, crossing a majority of Brazil's states, piercing into several of them over and over again.

The fundamental object of the Prestes Column was to arouse the civilian population of the backlands against the then dominant regime. In this it failed. Almost everywhere it was met by the fierce though ill-directed opposition of the local people, organized into a hastily recruited militia. It never got control of any of the country's major cities and thus made little contact with the labor movement or other discontented elements in the urban communities.

However, it was not entirely a failure. It built up a *"mistica"* about the members of the group and particularly around Prestes, which was still a force in Brazilian political life a quarter of a century later. Prestes was greeted by even the hostile press as a military genius, being compared with Napoleon, Caesar and Alexander. He was dubbed the "Knight of Hope" and became virtually a legendary figure. The lesser members of the Column shared in this buildup. They developed an esprit-de-corps and a unity which was to be largely responsible for the Revolution of 1930, and won the respect and loyalty of large elements of the civilian population, particularly in rural areas.

Those who participated in the activities of the Prestes Column were the men who were to dominate the country's political life after the Revolution of 1930. . . . The Revolution of 1930 was largely the work of the Tenentes. . . .

However, the Tenentes were not successful in working out a consistent program or in organizing a Tenentista Party. This was a great tragedy: they could not organize, on a civilian plane, to establish a party which would rally the forces of unrest and discontent with the old regime existent in Brazil at that time. Nor were they able to develop a consistent body of doctrine, such as Haya de la Torre and his friends in Peru evolved during the 1920s.

Their ideas, however, evolved rapidly in the months following the October 1930 Revolution. During the period of the Prestes Column, and even during the preparation

of the 1930 revolt, they had had a simple political program, summed up in the old slogan, "a new broom sweeps
clean," but with little reference to social issues. Once in
power, however, they quickly became aware that they
must come to grips with social problems.

During the time of the Prestes Column the magazine,
"*5 de Julho*," which spoke for the Column, expressed the
ideas of the Revolutionaries thus:

> Reasons: financial and economic disorder; exorbitant
> taxes; administrative dishonesty; lack of justice; per-
> version of the vote; subornation of the press; political
> persecution; disrespect for the autonomy of the states;
> lack of social legislation; reform of the constitution
> under the state of siege. Ideals: to assure a regime
> loyal to the republican Constitution; to establish free
> primary instruction and professional and technical
> training throughout the country; to assure liberty
> of thought; to unify justice, putting it under the
> aegis of the Supreme Court; to unify the treasury;
> to assure municipal liberty; to castigate the defraud-
> ers of the patrimony of the people; to abolish the
> anomaly whereby professional politicians become
> prosperous at the expense of the public purse; rigor-
> ous economy of public moneys in keeping with
> efficient aid to the economic forces of the country.

This was not in any sense a "socialistic" program. By the
outbreak of the 1930 Revolution the leaders of the Tenentes
had developed somewhat in their thinking on social problems. Thus Juarez Távora, in arguing against Prestes'
endorsement of communist methods early in 1930, says of
his former chief's position:

> One sees between the lines of his recent manifesto
> a frank revolt against the injustices of the present

bourgeois organization of our society. He is not in
agreement with the monstrosity whereby an insignificant minority of bourgeois potentates . . . op-
presses the great majority who work and produce.

Távora agrees with Prestes' indictment of contemporary
Brazilian society, saying that he "recognizes the inequity of
this order of things under which the proletarian majority
labors," but he does not feel that it can be righted by
"upsetting the existing order." His prescription for the
situation was "proportional representation of all social
classes" and some less fundamental changes.

One contemporary Brazilian commentator on Tenentismo, writing a few years after the 1930 Revolution, maintained that the Tenente program in the Revolution was
"social democratic" and noted that it included demands
for government recognition of trade unions and cooperatives; labor legislation, including minimum wage and maxi-
mum hour laws and anti-child labor legislation. The Tenentes also generally favored nationalization of the mines and
of foreign trade, and a division of the latifundia, that is, an
agrarian reform. They sought, says this writer, a "moderate,
petty-bourgeois capitalism."

. . . However, although some of the things in which
the Tenentes believed were enacted after the Revolution
of 1930, as a group they were never able to establish a
political organization which could assure the orderly enactment of the program in which they believed. This failure
to establish a Tenente political party was due in part to
the fact that they had come to power in alliance with
essentially conservative elements, such as Vargas himself,
Arturo Bernardes, the old-line Paulista opposition, and
other groups; and these conservative elements attempted
to play down as much as possible the role which the
Tenentes had played in the 1930 Revolution. . . .

15

Richard M. Morse

Urban Growth
and Cultural Ferment

*Another form of urban protest in the 1920s was
the Week of Modern Art. It was organized by young
writers and artists in São Paulo during the very year*
tenentismo *found its first expression in Rio de Janeiro.
Professor Richard M. Morse of Yale University is
the author of a history of São Paulo. In the following selection he examines the frenetic growth of that
city after 1880, the accompanying philistinism, and
the eventual reaction of youthful intellectuals. Brazilian* modernismo *spanned the interwar years and laid
the basis for that nation's continued cultural vigor.
The movement forms one of the most important
chapters in Brazilian intellectual history.*

The surge of city growth began in the 1880s. Between
1886 and 1893 the population increased threefold, from
44,030 to 129,409. Railways, fanning out from São Paulo,

From Richard M. Morse, "São Paulo Since Independence: A Cultural Interpretation," *Hispanic American Historical Review*, XXXIV
(November 1954), 419–444. The following selection is from pp.
430–437. Reprinted by permission of the author and the publisher,
Duke University Press.

gave it dominion over a farflung coffee frontier. Coffee wealth subsidized the advent of tens of thousands of European immigrants, many of whom were drawn to the *paulista* capital, where nascent industries and rapid urbanization offered livelier promises than did the *fazendas*. In short, the city now exhibited a complex of energies which guaranteed it the hallmarks of a metropolis: industry, commerce, public utilities, banking, ornamental parks and buildings, cultural diversions and a fast-expanding populace. Little demand existed for the political and philosophic speculation of earlier decades—except perhaps when fragments of federalist theory were exhumed to chide the government for siphoning off *paulista* wealth. So confident was the city of the rewards and inevitability of its progress that, in contrast to Rio de Janeiro, it scarcely offered a foothold to the formal cult of positivism.

When after a thirty-year absence, the former law student "Junius" returned to São Paulo in 1882, he was struck by its quick, noisy tempo of life. Earlier at mid-century, upper-class families had entered the streets only to attend church or to make formal visits, and were always escorted by the paterfamilias. Cafés did not exist, and if a youth went to a restaurant for beer or even "agua com assucar," he was held as extravagant and perhaps immoral. So few were the carriages that citizens hurried to their windows to identify the owner of any that passed. Now, however, in 1882, there were countless pedestrians, including unescorted ladies, and the streets reverberated with the constant passage of streetcars. Junius was amazed by the profusion of shops and the luxury of their wares; by the availability of toys and musical instruments, foreign wines and tobacco, foreign books and journals; by the ease with which a man or woman could acquire a complete Parisian wardrobe or grooming; by the resplendent Grande Hotel, which had no equal in Brazil and was reminiscent of Europe's best. He was impressed by the new suburbs, rail-

ways, public buildings and the illumination and activity of
streets after dark.

The change which had come over the city is further
pointed up in the comments of two travelers, made some
fifty years apart. In 1855 the American J. C. Fletcher
ascribed "a more intellectual and a less commercial air" to
São Paulo, where "you do not hear the word *dinheiro*
constantly ringing in your ear, as at Rio de Janeiro." In
1909 the Frenchman Denis remarked that: "The society
of São Paulo is less given to literature, diction and eloquence than that of Rio; though one feels it to be more
active, São Paulo is not the capital of Brazilian letters. It
is impassioned over economic questions."

With the passage of urban Brazil into the republican era
Gilberto Freyre associates a denial of the humanistic and
intimately experienced Afro-Portuguese heritage. Family
heirlooms of silver and jacarandá were auctioned off to
foreigners and replaced by more modish acquisitions from
Europe. "The bad Portuguese habits of picking the teeth
in public and of spitting noisily on the floor" were outlawed by a new Frenchified élite. Classics and humanities
yielded to practical, technical disciplines. Children were
baptized Newton, Jefferson and Edison instead of Ulysses,
Demosthenes and Cicero. Harsh English words like "trust,"
"funding-loan" and "deficit" were injected into the vocabu-
lary. One spoke of the abstract complexities of coffee
valorization, but no longer of the "valorization of the
Brazilian man—of the man and of the people."

In such an atmosphere cultural pursuits were subordinated to the order of material progress, becoming an ad-
junct rather than a dimension of city life. Practitioners of
the arts were often professional virtuosi from Europe, who,
as dramatic and operatic performers for example, left
students and townspeople in only a spectator's rôle. To
patronize the arts was an emblem of social distinction or,
at best, a sentimental indulgence. In 1887 dilettantes were

reported to have arrived at a concert of chamber music in São Paulo "with plenty of strong coffee in their stomachs to resist the temptations of Morpheus (sic!), God of classical music." They were "deeply versed in dissonant harmonies; all of them perform a duet with the players, for if the latter play some Hungarian hodgepodge in Ti, the former with falsetto voices snore in Sol."

Art served to advertise wealth, as did the palatial but hybrid styles of the new residences (*palacetes*) along aristocratic Avenida Paulista. By the 1870s the time-honored *taipa* construction was looked upon as drab and rustic, and use of the once-romantic *rótula* was officially banned. By the next decade, as the architect Ricardo Severo later recalled, immigrant Italian stuccoers were introducing:

> . . . sculptured ornament applied to completely smooth façades without discretion, architectural composition or minimal esthetic sense. . . .
>
> The thread of tradition was wholly lost in the eclectic labyrinth of foreign influences. . . . Heed was no longer paid to the physical milieu and the orographic conformation of its terrain and local countryside, to the social scene with its uses and customs, its habits of family and collective life; and the structural forms inherent in the materials of the country were not forth-rightly developed.

The tycoon of this new architecture was Francisco de Paula Ramos de Azevedo (1851–1928). More engineer than architect, more entrepreneur than engineer, Ramos de Azevedo, with his associates, set up a dictatorship over the city's taste that has only recently begun to crumble; his "style" was pinchbeck, derivative and best described as promiscuous eclecticism with leanings toward the Renaissance. The ostentatious way of life for which the *palacete* stood is depicted in the daydreams of Lenita, the sensual heroine of Júlio Ribeiro's *A carne* (1887); the novel itself, a social-Darwinian jeremiad lacking art or compassion, is indicative of the times.

The burgeoning metropolis which has been described soon engulfed the once-prominent student body of the Law Academy. The *bacharel* degree, now a mere entrée to a niche in the bureaucratic urban order, no longer entailed pioneer responsibilities for marking out horizons of national life. As one professor remarked in 1888, most students hoped only for "legal admission into certain careers," some going so far as to yield all faith in their own abilities and place all hope in "nepotism and political protection."

Student writers of the 1880s formed beer-drinking cliques, displayed studied eccentricities and produced languid poetry of an escapist or ornamental nature. Until well into the twentieth century their literary circles were characterized by bohemian affectation. Such a group was that of Ricardo Mendes Gonçalves of the class of 1905, who lived in a yellow chalet called *O Minarete* with the future writer and publicist José Bento Monteiro Lobato, the future anthropologist Arthur Ramos and other young literati. They were known as "a cauçalha," Gonçalves was "o cão que ladra à lua," and none—in their student days at least — showed traces of the *modernismo* which is now to be discussed.

It was, according to Mário de Andrade, in about 1916 that "the conviction of a new art" came to "a little group of *paulista* intellectuals." Perhaps the single most stimulating influence was the exhibit in that year of the bold expressionist paintings of the young artist Anita Malfatti, who had just returned from Europe and from studies in the United States. It was not long before another painter, Emiliano di Cavalcanti, the poet Guilherme de Almeida and the novelist Oswald de Andrade were holding daily

conversations in the bookstore *O Livro*. Soon others joined
them. Authors read new poems and books; more exhibits
were held; musicians played new compositions. And the
idea of the public sessions that were organized in February 1922, as the *Semana de Arte Moderna* gradually took
shape.

The *Semana* represented the efforts of a group of young
men and women who, with diverse media and outlooks,
had found a common enterprise in trying to penetrate and
render into form the flux of modern life. Most or all of
them had been born since 1890 and were thus the first
generation to have experienced São Paulo as a metropolis
from their earliest years. Although certain of them eventually defined the artist's social mission with uncompromising rigidity, one of the *modernistas'* primary services was
to reincorporate art and society. Art, as indicated above,
had come to mean virtuosity; the virtuoso was isolated
from his milieu by a routinized vision of it and from fellow
artists by the competitiveness of their interchangeable
talents. The *modernistas* were once again, like the roman-
ticists of 1850, artists-in-community. During the early
years "we were really pure and free, disinterested," Mário
de Andrade later wrote. "No one thought of sacrifice, no
one treasured the unintelligible, no one imagined himself
precursor or martyr."

The *Semana* was celebrated in the Municipal Theater,
an imitation of the Parisian *Opéra* which stood for the
very cultural attitudes that *modernismo* sought to explode.
A few offerings, such as the piano-playing of Guiomar de
Novaes and the music of the young composer Heitor Villa
Lôbos, were appreciatively received by the public. Writers
and painters, however, elicited a furore reminiscent of
New York's Armory Show of 1913. Scandalous gossip
about them was invented and circulated. Canvases by Lasar
Segall—a young Russian-born, German-trained expression-
ist who had first exhibited in São Paulo in 1913—and by
Anita Malfatti were attacked with canes. Readings by poets

and novelists were rendered inaudible by hoots and catcalls. *O Estado de São Paulo* suggested that the *modernistas* had planted claques to aggravate the uproar, and, certainly, the poet Menotti del Picchia went out of his way to provoke tumult in a speech that began:

> The automobiles of the planets careen dizzily along the highway of the Milky Way. . . . The constellations play in a jazzband of light, syncopating the harmonic dance of the spheres. The sky seems a huge electric billboard that God set up on high to advertise for eternity His omnipotence and glory.
> . . . This is the style that traditionalists expect of us. . . . What an error! Nothing more orderly and peaceful than this vanguard group, freed of traditional totemism, alive to the policed, American life of today.

What was striking about the young *modernistas* was not, however, their insolence and iconoclasm but their self-consciousness and missionary dedication. This was reflected in their first literary review, which referred to the *Semana* as a medical necessity: "Damp, chilled, rheumatic with a tradition of artistic tears, we made up our minds. Surgical operation. Excision of the lachrymal glands."

That the 1922 group had not been doctrinally or stylistically unified was evident after 1924, when manifestoes and magazines of such cliques as *Pau Brasil, Verdamarelismo* and *Antropofagia* began to counteract European currents with nativist and nationalistic appeals. As 1930 drew near and political restlessness increased, artistic programs were infiltrated by political credos. Novels by such writers as the self-styled "mural" novelist Oswald de Andrade and fascist-oriented Plínio Salgado challenged the supremacy initially enjoyed by poetry, since they were better vehicles for social concern.

After 1930 it is hard to speak of *modernismo* as a single

phenomenon. Even among the non-political, the ramifica-
tion of interest and emphasis became extreme. There were
nativists, Europeanizers, Americanizers. Some continued to
shock the bourgeois; others courted the underprivileged;
others created worlds of private symbolism. There was
increasing exchange with other cultural regions of Brazil.
There was interplay between the arts and research disciplines. For many, *modernismo* became social anthropology;
recovery of neglected folklore; study of Brazil's social,
economic and political institutions; ethnology and philol-
ogy; or literary criticism. The philosophically inclined were
attracted to the less schematic, less deterministic systems
(notably the Germanic thought diffused by Ortega y
Gasset) and to an eclectic, historically oriented quest for
a Brazilian "ontology." Still another *modernista* concern
was with rehabilitating and preserving documents, art
works and architecture of the past, a task in large part
assumed by the local branch of the Serviço do Patrimônio
Histórico e Artístico Nacional.

Those who kept to artistic creativity displayed similar
diversity. Of one salon of painters in the 1930s the critic
Sérgio Milliet said that it represented "a state of spirit"
rather than "a school." "And that state of spirit," he
pointed out, "is that of our contradictory century, pained
and joyful, troubled and mystical, disillusioned but none-
theless constructive." Likewise the literary reviews assumed
an attitude of serious, pluralistic inquiry. In 1941 *Clima*
announced its title to signify a " 'climate' of curiosity,
interest and intellectual ventilation." The editors had mul-
tifarious interests but looked beyond the encyclopedism of
positivists and evolutionists; they hoped to mediate among
the realms of the modern mind and to avoid facile system-
atizing. This exploratory, self-critical phase of *modernismo*
was in some measure a response to an atmosphere of world
crisis and to the disillusion engendered by the inadequate
leadership and ideals of the *paulista* Revolution of 1932.

Though virtually unrepresented at the *Semana de Arte Moderna,* architecture has in recent years come to be the clearest manifestation of the urban, social dimensions of *modernismo.* By the 1930s, following the example of Rino Levi and Austrian-born Bernardo Rudofsky, architects began to discriminate among modern techniques and solutions from abroad with an eye to the particular needs of São Paulo. Cinemas, hospitals and workers' communities were boldly designed for the comfort and movement of large concentrations of people. Attention was paid to the seasonal cold which distinguishes the climate from that of Rio de Janeiro, and buildings were faced to catch the afternoon rather than the morning sun. Office and apartment skyscrapers were stripped of stuccoed embellishment, and the structures made possible by the lightness and flexibility of reinforced concrete were increasingly explored. Walls came to be thought of not as unwieldy supports of brick but as ductile partitions, or as an epidermis mediating between living-space and outer environment.

Levi and Rudofsky have designed private residences that are as striking as the public buildings—with their sliding partitions that allow house and garden to interpenetrate; their modulations of contour, volume, and light; their accentuation of regional building materials; and their plain walls, set off by the shifting outlines of semitropical foliage. It might almost be said that the handsome country *chácara* of a century ago has been recreated in the idiom of the modern age.

The *modernista* movement, becoming ever more labyrinthine, may be said to have lasted some twenty-five years; its terminus was perhaps marked by the death of Mário de Andrade in 1945, or perhaps by the appearance of a group of young poets whose skilled, hermetic verse has been advertised as *neo-modernista.* One cannot say, however, that *modernismo* has been "superseded." Like romanticism, it was a "state of spirit," not a body of dogma, and therefore an open, not a closed system. And, it may be surmised, the roots of *modernismo* are more deeply struck than were those of romanticism; its ramifications have been more diverse and conscientiously explored. It appears to be a threshold to cultural maturity, and to an era of organic, less spasmodic cultural change.

III

Brazil Since 1930

16

André Carrazzoni

The Achievements
of Getúlio Vargas

*The figure of Getúlio Vargas dominates the history
of Brazil from 1930 to 1954, and his memory still
hovers over its politics. He ruled as provisional President or dictator from 1930 to 1934, was elected constitutional President in 1934, took over dictatorial
powers again in 1937, and was not overthrown until
1945. He was then elected President by an overwhelming majority in an open election in 1950; and
he ruled constitutionally until his suicide in 1954.
Two of the leading parties before 1964 were virtually
his creation.*

*As in the case of Pedro II, the question most often
raised about him is whether he contributed to the
nation's progress and, if so, to what degree. No final
answer will ever be given, for it would depend upon
a knowledge of what would have happened if the
Vargas phenomenon had never appeared. What is
certain is that Brazil has been transformed in the
period since 1930. Perhaps Vargas was an effect
rather than a cause of these changes, but the selection*

Translated and printed from André Carrazzoni, *Getúlio Vargas*
(Rio de Janeiro: José Olympio, 1939), pp. 270–275, 281–283, by
permission of the publisher.

*presented here (published at the peak of his political
career) pictures him as the creator of the new order.
The author of this article was the journalist André
Carrazzoni, who followed Vargas from Rio Grande
do Sul to Rio de Janeiro and there became the editor
of the newspaper* A Noite.

Surveying the achievement of the first three years of his
provisional government [1930–1933], Getúlio Vargas could
point to new benchmarks in administrative, political, social,
economic, and financial matters. In these three years he
did what he could, undoing the errors of the past, improving the present, and banishing the shadows from a fearful
future.

Within the limits of a small budget, he sought to satisfy
the aspirations of the army and navy by diminishing the
alarming disproportion between their technical and material
neglect and the minimum needs of national defense. We
were—and still are—practically an undefended country
open to all grasping ambitions "in this brutally antiromantic
age."

With the coffee crisis under control, he supported other
equally threatened agricultural products by a prudent
policy of public intervention, limiting production but allowing a margin for the spontaneous play of natural laws.

With regard to labor legislation, foreseeing the danger
of violent demands, he nationalized and organized labor
through the law of two-thirds Brazilian workers [in any
foreign company], through the law on paid vacations,
through the forty-eight-hour workweek, through the creation of mixed [labor] commissions (the first step toward
the establishment of the Labor Court system), through
the establishment of compulsory pension systems, through
the creation of orderly labor unions within and not without the state, and, finally, through measures to protect
women and children.

The same activity, always directed toward the most important problems, was evident in the building of port works, highways, railroads, airports, dams, and telephone and telegraph networks. In a country with more than 3 million square miles and a sparse demographic density, caught up in the process of assimilating waves of immigrants, the progress of civilization depends upon eliminating the wilderness. This is the primary purpose of the communications system. For this very reason it is a leitmotif of the Vargas administration. That timely formula of his, "interior unification of Brazil," is a response to the crying necessity to populate our countryside through the gradual conquest of the land by all life forces. The desert will give way to man and man will supplant it.

The era of progress that transforms Brazil after 1930 is to be, most of all, a triple function of the state: health, education, population. "Man," he said, "is the product of his habitat. To control nature is to improve social life. To conquer the land is to drain the swamps, to irrigate the arid regions, and to transform them into rich granaries. To combat intestinal disorders, endemic disease, inadequate hygienic conditions is to build capable and proud citizens" (Manifesto to the Nation, June 1934). The triangulation of Brazilian progress . . . rested on three reference points: to improve health, to broaden education, and to populate. . . .

During the three years reviewed before the Constituent Assembly [November 1933], Getúlio Vargas revealed the temperament and method of a born administrator. A worker of exceptional capacity, he never dealt with or solved a problem without first considering its social meaning and historical repercussion. The delegate of the revolution, he was aware of his responsibilities as a reformer. To reform was to operate upon the flesh of men, and, even more delicately, upon the very soul of the collectivity. The surgeon, however, knew how to avoid the pain of overly deep incisions and how to use the anesthetic of patience. . . .

As constitutional President [1934–1937] Getúlio Vargas devoted himself to maintaining the continuity of his program outlined during the revolutionary three years, despite onslaughts of all sorts. Obeying the rules of the constitutional game, he was often hindered, thwarted, and constrained by them. Nevertheless, he managed to work around the sophisms of this system by exercising his prestige over men and parties, relying upon his solid support in popular opinion. He bravely faced the vast number of old and new problems, some created by the very crisis of progress, others deepened by the procrastinating spirit of previous administrations. . . .

Among the most important actions of the constitutional phase were the drainage works of the lowlands in the state of Rio de Janeiro. . . . Getúlio Vargas may rightly be proud of offering his contemporaries such a proof of unparalleled administrative courage, giving economic and social worth to a strip of land measuring 7 square miles at the very doors of the capital. . . .

All sectors of federal administration felt the surge of healthy renovation. . . . The balance sheet of achievements and improvements of Getúlio Vargas' government is unprecedented in the history of the republic. The settlement regarding the foreign debt; . . . methodical development of social insurance with coverage broadened to include many groups and jobs; preliminary studies for the establishment of large-scale steel manufacture to take advantage of the mineral reserves of the country; electrification of the Brazil Central Railway; . . . are all additional new departures which characterize the Vargas government.

Afonso Arinos de Melo Franco

———◄◆►►———

Getúlio Vargas:
A More Caustic View

*Even today a discussion of the role of Getúlio
Vargas will inevitably provoke heated debate in
Brazil. The following selection captures the view of
the liberal, urbane, well-traveled elite, which found
Getúlio's violation of political liberties deeply disturbing. No credit is given to him for the economic
growth of the last thirty-odd years; some speakers go
on to say that, in fact, growth was not greater precisely because of his policies. The labor legislation
that he put through is dismissed because it served
his political ambitions. Admiration for his power of
survival is hastily countered by allusions to his non-
constitutional methods.*

*Afonso Arinos de Melo Franco, the author of this
selection, is a distinguished jurist, political leader,
professor, historian, and ambassador. His biography*

This selection is from pp. 154–156 of Afonso Arinos de Melo
Franco, "The Tide of Government: From Colony to Constitutional
Democracy," Richard M. Morse, trans., *The Atlantic Monthly*,
CXCVII, No. 2 (February 1956), 152–156. Reprinted from *The
Atlantic Monthly*, February 1956. Copyright © 1956, by Intercul-
tural Publications, Inc., New York, New York. Reprinted with
permission of the copyright owner.

of his father, Um estadista da república (*1955*), *is also a brilliant survey of the history of the First Republic.*

. . . [The First Republic] drew its main strength from the governors of the states, and especially of the two big ones, Minas Gerais and São Paulo: Between these two existed a sort of gentlemen's agreement regulating an almost predestined alternation of control over the most important positions in the federal government.

Circumstances which there is no space to enumerate caused this agreement to collapse in 1930. São Paulo and Minas became alienated and then hostile over the presidential election of that year, and the *mineiro* politicians decided to look for an ally in the state which was third-ranking in political importance and which, in terms of fighting spirit and the militancy of its sons, led the whole nation: Rio Grande do Sul.

The entrance upon the scene of the impetuous *gaúchos* —led there by the *mineiros,* who had won renown for their prudence and their mastery of political stratagem— had the effect after 1930 of completely upsetting the familiar historical patterns of the republican era. An important agent of that transformation was the personal influence of Getúlio Vargas who, after leaving the presidency of Rio Grande, became successively the candidate of the alliance of *mineiros* and *gaúchos* (1930), leader of the national revolution, and dictator (1930–34), constitutional President (1934–37), dictator once again (1937–45), President once again (1951–54), and, in brief, the central figure on the stage for nearly a quarter of a century.

The intricate personal history of Getúlio Vargas united three elements that made him, if not an authentic revolutionary, at least a man wholly indifferent to the fate of legal institutions, which existed merely as obstacles to the fulfillment of his enormous ambition for power. Those three elements were *gauchismo,* militarism, and positivism. As a *gaúcho* from an old family of the southern frontier, Vargas carried in his blood the mixed tradition of the guerrilla wars of the pampas, and of a social life that was regulated more by the arms of the dominant patriarchy than by effective law and order. A soldier in his youth, Vargas did not continue his military career; from his barracks days he did however keep his taste for the methods of direct action, of radical intervention in political life, and for eliminating the lengthy and at times confusing delays generic to the functioning of democratic institutions. It should be pointed out that his interventionist militarism, from which the Empire was almost exempt and which became an influential factor only after the war with Paraguay, always had its main locus in the garrisons of Rio Grande do Sul. Finally, Vargas' family belonged to the Republican Party of Rio Grande, a party founded under the auspices of the political philosophy of Auguste Comte and nourished by its doctrines. Rio Grande was the Brazilian state in which positivism had its liveliest political repercussions. For that reason its constitution represented an unusual and immoderate brand of law by comparison with the other states, guaranteeing and encouraging the dictatorship of the executive over the other powers, a dictatorship that was in fact exercised for decades by President [i.e., governor] Borges de Medeiros—today [1956] still alive and over ninety—the chief and mentor of Vargas and of the whole generation of *gaúchos* which came to dominate Brazil in 1930.

To these elements of his background Vargas added personal qualities that contributed in large measure to his historical destiny. Keen intelligence, personal courage, serenity, deliberation in making decisions, a taste for listening, and a talent for keeping quiet (in contrast with the

Latin penchant for oratory), a startling lack of sentiments, either of hate or of affection, that guarded him against passionate impulses—these were some of his character traits. Although he was personally honest, his general cynicism and, in some measure, his scorn for the men who habitually surround those in power left him wholly unscrupulous in his choice of means for coaxing support from anyone who might be necessary or useful to his ambitions. This was the most unfortunate mark of his character and the one which, accentuated by the weariness natural for his age, carried his final constitutional government to the phase of disintegration and corruption in which it tragically foundered.

As a public figure Vargas was a patriot; he sincerely loved his land and his people. His ambition for power, his love for the game of politics, and his irrepressible bent for demagogy perverted those noble sentiments into unfortunate excesses. His love of country led him gradually into a kind of elementary nationalism; at first, perhaps, this served merely as a useful weapon, but it came to be the natural characteristic of a man who, in spite of his intelligence, was not truly cultured and lacked a broad vision of the world—and who had never left Brazil except for formal visits of a few days to neighboring countries. His love of the people, which became manifest only after he had been chief executive for several years, was transformed into deliberate rabble-rousing—the so-called "populism" of Vargas; its principal aim was to capture, by instilling fear of the masses, the support of the elite and of the military, who he felt were becoming alienated by the universal suspicion [in 1954] that he might be planning to restore the dictatorship. . . .

With the diversification of the Brazilian economy, and particularly with its strides toward industrialization, the economic pattern of the first Republic (1889–1930), dominated by coffee-planting, underwent profound change.

The slogan of the times had been: "Brazil is basically an agricultural country." In certain respects this ceased to be true. Although it is a fact that coffee continues to account for the lion's share of our foreign exchange, it is equally true that, in the domestic market, industrial production has acquired a social and even economic importance substantially larger than that of coffee.

This diversification of the economy made impossible— in a free country, as Brazil has nearly always been—the onetime political unity of the state parties under the command of state presidents who were more or less submissive to the President of the Republic. Significantly, it was in São Paulo, the most wealthy and progressive state, that the new economic and social forces began [before 1930] to find expression through new political organizations, distinct from the old statewide republican parties. At first these new opposition parties represented the demands of the liberal urban bourgeoisie, such as elimination of electoral fraud, closer control of administrative acts, a curb on the powers of the President of the Republic, and extension of the inherent powers of the Congress.

The vigorous and powerful personalities of the last three Presidents of the first Republic, Epitácio Pessoa (1919–22), Artur Bernardes (1922–26), and Wáshington Luís (1926–30), all of them committed to an obstinate defense of the traditional presidential prerogatives which were now being threatened, aggravated the conflict instead of allowing the concessions that would have lessened it. The national revolution of 1930 broke out and swept into power the *gaúcho,* Getúlio Vargas.

Vargas, who was leader more in name than in fact of the triumphant revolutionary forces, little by little made himself the fulcrum of events by virtue of both his qualities and his defects. By 1934 the change was complete. Having made no commitments of any sort and cherishing the desire, after the example of his master, Borges de Medeiros, of keeping himself indefinitely in power, he became ever more convinced that the liberalism of the revolution represented merely the thinking of an elite. The masses, he felt, awakened by industrialization and other factors, were making social demands of a very different nature; these were not to be confused with the legalistic ideals of the revolution of 1930 that he had stood for. The more he became aware of this fact, the more Vargas identified himself with these new longings and disengaged himself from his former liberal involvements. With characteristic acumen and intelligence, he began to establish himself as the knight of the new crusade.

It was, indeed, not true that social progress could be attained only at the expense of freedom. To maintain himself in power, however, Vargas increasingly associated his policy of meeting popular demands with anti-liberal practices. He was perhaps truly convinced at the end of his life that the future of the Brazilian people depended upon his remaining in power and that therefore to oppose his tenure was the same as to work against bettering the living standard of the people. After the defeat of world fascism, however, it became impossible to keep up this equivocation in a country with Brazil's liberal traditions. The liberal demands of privileged groups were decisively confirmed by the people, and after 1943 one could predict an early end of the dictatorship. Vargas was turned out in 1945 by the armed forces, who were now thoroughly converted to the democratic cause by the allied victory to which they had contributed in Italy—but only to find himself spectacularly returned to power in 1950. This, in contrast to his election to the presidency in 1934 by the Constituent Assembly, was his first elevation to the office by a popular vote, although the election was more nearly a plebiscite in favor of a single man and against the organized parties.

Restored to power, and still in possession of his nimble intelligence and his talent for accommodation, Vargas soon perceived that his tenure depended upon other elements than that of force. When he had established the dictatorship in 1937 he had done so with the support of the military, who were hostile to communism and impressed with the success of the Italian and German dictatorships. In 1950 the situation was different. The armed forces were sincerely and firmly committed to the democratic camp and would never again serve as an instrument to destroy the Constitution. Vargas therefore turned to the proletariat as the *point d'appui* of his perennial ambition for power; and the indefatigable politico began to make use of the labor unions, which were now converted into mere cat's-paws of the palace; strikes arranged by his most intimate agents; and the direct pressure of the masses upon existing institutions. However, this new brand of action, or rather, of conspiracy, demanded methods of corruption and violence which soon became public knowledge and caused widespread repugnance.

Vargas, who had never cast off his *gaúcho* habits of the *guerrilheiro* and of the provisional troop commander, resided in his palace like certain princes of the Renaissance, surrounded by his little army of personal guards. These men, recruited from the common people, were one of the most important agents of his downfall. Getting on in years, strangely isolated although constantly in company, badly informed, possibly weary and bereft of faith, Vargas was little by little losing control of the situation which had crystallized around him. Then, when the crime took place which had been plotted inside the palace itself with the aim of eliminating Carlos Lacerda, the most notable newspaperman of the opposition—a crime in which the journalist escaped and a young air corps officer lost his life—an intolerable state of affairs within the government was suddenly revealed to the startled country. It is only fair to make clear that Vargas, although blameworthy for that state of affairs, was not responsible for the crime itself or for the more unsavory aspects of his environment. His vehement condemnation of the "river of mud" flowing through the cellar of his palace, made to an intimate colleague during his last days, allows the belief that his surprise at this reality of his own making was almost as great as that of his enemies. Psychologically oppressed by such numerous and diverse emotions, in August 1954, Vargas turned to suicide.

A man's self-destruction is always a mysterious act which, in combination with the psychological pressures of the moment, distant and more profound influences may be expected to precipitate. Vargas' suicide, which produced a world sensation, caused tremendous shock in Brazil itself. His friends and his enemies gave contradictory explanations. Probably both were right in much of what they said. It seems certain that Vargas killed himself so as to defend the Constitution, under which he was the chief executive, and so as not to yield to a dismissal which, in spite of the euphemism of forced "vacation," he felt would be permanent. He furthermore wished to save the lives of his most devoted friends, who were at his side in the palace and who might have been sacrificed had they offered armed resistance to the popular and military demonstrations that urged the President's resignation.

In addition, however, it must be recognized that through his suicide Vargas wished also to redeem himself in the eyes of history. By killing himself he became dissociated from the crimes and blunders which had engulfed his government, and thus assured his survival for posterity. Had he lived out the few remaining years of his life he might have been forgotten by the distant future. Therefore his death was a kind of resurrection. It was most probably this last consideration which fortified his spirit—the spirit of a man who was, before all else, a public figure.

18

José Valladares

The Art of the Tropics

The artistic innovations of the 1920s left their mark on painting as well as literature. Some thirty years later it was possible to survey the subsequent work of several artists whose achievement may be termed outstanding. José Valladares (1917–1959), who wrote the following selection, was an art critic and historian; he taught at the University of Bahia until his death in a plane crash.

The belated introduction of the Brazilian public to a type of painting that was not academic probably occurred first at the exhibition of Lasar Segall's work in São Paulo in 1913. Nine years later, this same city was host to the famous *Semana de Arte Moderna* (Modern Art Week), which was chiefly a literary event but which had far-reaching repercussions among the fine arts as well. During the next fifteen years, Brazilian painting attained an international level and came into its own.

This selection is from pp. 154–156 of José Valladares, "The Art of the Tropics: Painting and Sculpture in Brazil," *The Atlantic Monthly*, CXCVII, No. 2 (February 1956), 126–127. Reprinted from *The Atlantic Monthly*, February 1956. Copyright © 1956, by Intercultural Publications, Inc., New York, New York. Reprinted with permission of the copyright owner.

For Brazil, this meant giving up the traditional academic teaching of Europe and experimenting with a type of painting more closely related to its own life. To be explicit, the ingredients of the Brazilian melting pot are more highly integrated than, for instance, the disparate ethnic strains of the United States. The Moorish, African, and indigenous Indian elements have been amalgamated with the European heritage, so that today one finds in Brazilian art a unique tropical flavor, a combination of the Portuguese tradition of opulent design and the native propensity for the picturesque.

Fauvism, cubism, futurism, primitivism, and surrealism began to make their way into the studios and discussions of Brazilian artists in the 1920s. The new conventions of taste and sensibility in a very short time proved to be better adapted to the depiction of Brazilian scenery, people, customs, and the national soul than the strict middle-of-the-road formalisms of nineteenth-century academic art.

Some years ago it was observed that modern Brazilian painting was split into two schools, one in São Paulo and one in Rio. The division stems from different approaches to painting, a difference in subject matter and local flavor. The *Paulistas* are more concerned with spiritual values and with workmanship, and they very often reflect the industrial, grayish, somber atmosphere of their fast-growing city; while the *Cariocas* tend toward a type of painting that is more monumental, more decorative, and related to the bright colors and sunny vistas of their environment. During the last few years, cities like Pôrto Alegre, Belo Horizonte, Recife, and Salvador have also become small art centers where painters admire but do not depend on the examples set by their colleagues in Rio and São Paulo.

Like other countries, Brazil has a group of painters who possess definite personal characteristics and a style which distinguishes them from the adepts of internationalism in art. They range from a primitive like Heitor dos

Prazeres or José Antônio da Silva to a master in composition and drawing like Portinari; from a realist like Pancetti to an abstractionist like Cícero Dias. Some, like Djanira, are intensely aware of local color, while others, like Guignard, use colors that are less local but very expressive of the subject.

Our best painter today, a man whose name and importance have been internationally recognized for many years, is Cândido Portinari, who was born in 1903 in Brodowski, São Paulo, of Italian parents and who now lives in Rio. His works have already appeared in textbooks on the history of art, and he was considered one of the few New World painters worth discussing in the recent *Dictionnaire de la Peinture Moderne.* The exceptional quality of Portinari's painting largely derives from his mastery of design and his innate feeling for monumental composition. On such good foundations he builds color to a surface of richness and brilliance, in fresco as well as in tempera and oil. There is dramatic feeling in his work, but it is conveyed through space and light rather than through actual gestures. His justly famous frescoes at the Hispanic Foundation of the Library of Congress in Washington, as well as those in the Ministry of Education in Rio de Janeiro, his gigantic canvases, *First Mass in Brazil* or the *Tiradentes,* all testify to his wise understanding of the problems of a bare wall. Portinari's work has revealed a very obvious tenderness for the people of his own country; he is the painter who has most faithfully and convincingly represented the Indian, the Negro, the *mestiço,* and the white man who have made Brazil what it is. He has used these typical figures in compositions that show the basic activities of Brazilian economic life, past and present, in a way far more eloquent than any artist before him. Canvases by Portinari are found in several European and American museums and private collections. At present, he is working on two huge allegories of war and peace, which are to decorate one of the rooms of the United Nations Building in New York.

It would be erroneous to pretend that the work of Lasar Segall (born in 1890, in Vilna, Russia, and living in São Paulo) has the same Brazilian meaning that we find in Portinari. His paintings belong to a school that pays more attention to interior problems than to the world around him. As a representative of the expressionist group, Segall's concern with the intricacies of the human spirit has very often led him to subjects that are autobiographical, and hence his painting offers a special insight into the experience of the many immigrants who have come from distant lands to live in Brazil. His paintings inspire a deep admiration for a sincere artist who has devoted all his talent and energy to the constant improvement of his work, experimenting in different techniques with the utmost care, and always motivated by his desire for the perfection of his art and by a noble although discreet sense of human brotherhood. Although he is chiefly an easel painter, he has done a few large canvases. In these compositions every single detail is treated as if it were an isolated painting. Houses, street scenes, his family, friends and unknown people, landscapes and animals, all these subjects have been interpreted by Segall with great sympathy and a sure hand. His complete works make a truthful picture of the reactions of a sensitive person to the problem of modern man in Brazil.

A precursor who should be mentioned along with Segall is Tarsila do Amaral, who not only was familiar with the school of Paris where she studied—the influence of [Fernand] Léger being strong at the time—but also spent a year in New York. She thus brought an international point of view to Brazil in the twenties. This was rejected at first by certain dominant figures in the intellectual life of the country—notably the writer Monteiro Lobato—but her sincerity and true artistic personality ultimately won the day, and her technique came to be used more and more in a Brazilian manner. Two other colleagues, also widely traveled, Flávio de Carvalho and Oswald Andrade Filho, helped in other ways to enrich the new artistic climate.

Alberto Guignard (born in 1893, now living in Belo Horizonte) is a painter of candid reality. A nervous but clear design is the most effective element in his art, and it bespeaks a quick rhythm that reflects his own personality. Less preoccupied with the problems of society than Portinari and Segall, he transmits a sense of enjoyment and affection for the Brazilian scene. He is also a teacher of great influence, whose craftsmanlike approach to the problems of painting has attracted many students.

With Emiliano di Cavalcanti (born in 1897 in Rio and living in São Paulo) we come to one of the members of the old guard of modern painting in Brazil. In the early twenties, he was already one of the most talked-of artists in the country. A well-organized exhibition of his work would show how much he has evolved from a rather crude Fauvism to a type of painting related to cubism but full of personal discoveries. His favorite subject is the Brazilian *mestiço* and the everyday worker. In bright colors, expertly combined, he has peopled Brazilian painting with hundreds of sensuous women and violent men in a way paralleled by some of the country's novelists. One may like these creatures or not, but they are strong personalities.

Many Latin Americans have more than one string to their bow, and therefore José Pancetti's versatility should not surprise us. He is a poet who has also earned his living as a sailor in the Brazilian Navy, and his love of the sea is reflected in his marine painting, which has in fact made famous several sections of the Brazilian coast. Born a year before Portinari, and like him of Italian parentage, he has pursued his natural talent for landscape to the very heart of the Brazilian scene. His colors embrace a wide variety of nuances, since, although he is now a realist, he harks back to the post-impressionists. In his work nature undergoes a spontaneous purification.

Djanira (born a *Paulista* in 1914, now living in Rio) is another extremely personal painter. After years of serious study, she has developed a style which reveals training and knowledge but preserves her original interest in primitivism. Hers is the most beautiful decorative painting in Brazil. In some of her works small things which she loves, such as flowers, may grow to the size of human heads, while a disliked skyscraper may shrink to the height of a child's leg. In this world of magic, colors shine and sing, creating an intricate communion of man and nature.

The most consistent of Brazilian primitives is Heitor dos Prazeres, who was born in 1908 in Rio, where he still lives. His paintings often depict the artistic world, where he is also known as a composer of popular music, with a brush which prefers gay subjects like *samba* parties and weddings. An absolutely self-taught artist, he belongs to the ever growing group that has sprung up in many countries during recent decades of artists who are good in spite of their unprofessional backgrounds.

The abstractionist Cícero Dias, born in Rio (1908) and now living in France, keeps in touch with the inventions of the School of Paris. Despite this, his paintings are clearly the work of a man who cannot escape the color, culture, and feeling of his motherland. Enigmatic as it may seem, no painter has given a clearer picture of the atmosphere of northeastern Brazil than Cícero Dias with his abstract compositions.

Alfredo Volpi (born in 1896 in Italy and now settled in São Paulo), after a long and varied career, has finally come to a type of painting that is a sort of delicate, musical arabesque, based on the most rudimentary forms and filled with sophisticated colors. His canvases give the impression of deliberate naïveté but one cannot deny their charm. He has also designed tiles, a form of art which came to Brazil in colonial times with the Dutch and Portuguese and which is particularly appropriate to the tropical climate. In the 1940s, Paulo Rossi Osir of São Paulo undertook to revive this art and gathered around him a group of competent and interested artists. The validity of the project is reflected in its successful architectural use.

19

Leslie Lipson

Development, the Oligarchy, and Politics

*The conflict between the idealism of the constitu-
tion and the realities of political life returned to
haunt Brazil as soon as the Vargas dictatorship had
been overthrown. Professor Leslie Lipson of the University of California at Berkeley spent a year in
Brazil in 1953 while serving the United Nations. His
acute observations and tentative prognostications
took on special meaning a decade later. But the tensions—of which he speaks—created by modern
change within a traditional social structure are a
dominant theme throughout the last century of Brazil's history.*

The problems of present-day Brazil are the travail of a
people in the midst of a three-dimensional renovation.
Their economy, politics, and social structure are changing

From Leslie Lipson, "Government in Contemporary Brazil," *Ca-
nadian Journal of Economics and Political Science*, XXII (1956),
183–198. Reprinted by permission of the author and the publisher.

simultaneously, but at different speeds. Much the fastest transformation is the economic. Political alterations are slower. Social reconstruction is the slowest. The purpose of this paper is to analyze some of the contradictions that exist within the state when the economy propels it forward while the social order holds it back. What happens in politics when reform of government must be adjusted to a fast rate of economic change and a slow rate of social change? And can such reform be accomplished when foreign examples are invoked to displace ingrained traditions?

I

The character of Brazilian government is curiously akin to that of the new buildings which abound in the Copacabana suburb of Rio and elsewhere. The architect, a master of the modern idiom, has designed an imposing elevation to the street and an entrance of striking beauty. But, as one enters, much will be found in the finish of the interior, and in the services and maintenance, that conflicts with the external view. For periods of varying length, water will cease to flow from the faucets; electricity will be cut off; street drains may be inadequate to carry off rain and sewage; and, sooner or later, the *bichos*[1] will find their way in. A building may look a thing of beauty, but without the necessary utilities it will not be a joy forever to live in. So it is with Brazil's politics. The Constitution that has been in force since 1946 displays an attractive, modern front. It also proclaims many excellent aspirations. The institutions and processes, however, that lie behind and below do not, in some vital particulars, conform to the façade. The result is a *mélange* of incompatibilities which are fascinating to describe but frustrating to define.

---

[1] Meaning insects or vermin, with the added association of monsters and wonders.

The practicability of political reform must be construed in the light of a legacy from the past, in which certain facts stand prominently forth. Brazil's traditional form of government was rule by an oligarchy. This remained predominant by authoritarian methods, which were open to view on some occasions and skillfully cloaked on others. Even when independence was substituted for Portuguese colonialism (1822), and again later when slavery was abolished (1888) and a republic replaced the empire (1889), instead of a transfer of power to the mass of the population what occurred was an internal rearrangement and a relatively slight extension of the circle of privilege. Yet, though the ruling oligarchy has been authoritarian— like any little group that is tenacious of power—its temper has been more restrained, its techniques less brutal, than in most countries of the Latin American region. Brazil accomplished its independence with a minimum of bloodshed and disorder, and it was by peaceful means that slavery and the empire were abolished. Nor has Brazil been a prey to the series of revolutions and dictatorships which have stained the history of nearly all its neighbors. The major exception to this statement is the *coup d'état* of Getúlio Vargas in the 1930s. Yet in practice his power was somewhat moderated, not by institutional checks, but by the Brazilian flair for effective ridicule. The stings of a dictator are never so sharp when it is possible to laugh him out of office. It is, of course, true that the army has been a far from negligible factor in politics. Indeed, its leaders helped decisively to stabilize the infant republic during the 1890s and to terminate the Vargas régime in 1945. Similarly, in August 1954, the army and air force contributed powerfully to the events that culminated in Vargas' second enforced resignation and his subsequent suicide. Nevertheless, the military have generally preferred to hover in the background, keeping their influence discreetly veiled. The soldier's sword stays mostly in its scabbard.

But the prevalence of a supple oligarchy has not been maintained without challenge. Much of Brazil's political history in its thirteen decades of independence can be construed as a struggle between an authoritarian tradition, safeguarding the privileges of a few, and the liberalizing potential of representative democracy. To convert the rule of oligarchy into a government controllable by the majority is never an easy task, and obstacles are accentuated when the precedents that supply the stimulus to change are drawn principally from foreign lands. It has been unfortunate that the eminent Brazilians who have provided leadership in movements of constitutional and political reform have had to pluck their examples and inspiration from without, because their higher education and reading, and many of their political ideas, were derived to a large extent from foreign sources. They have, therefore, been vulnerable to the criticism that systems of government do not readily transplant and continue to be alien long after they have been imported. During the emperorship of that sage and benevolent monarch, Dom Pedro Segundo, there was an outward approximation of Brazilian institutions to British forms, an imitative tendency that was understandable at a time when British naval and economic influence was paramount. With Dom Pedro cast in the role of Queen Victoria, Brazil adopted the cabinet type of government and even applied the labels of Liberal and Conservative to its two leading political clusters.

It was equally understandable that with the embrace of republicanism Brazil should take its new model from a sister-republic. Consequently, the Constitution of 1890 reproduced—with its federalism, separation of branches, bicameral Congress, etc.—the essentials of the governmental structure of the United States. Rui Barbosa, the erudite statesman-jurist who contributed the lion's share of the drafting, is severely criticized by the social scientist, Oliveira Vianna, for extracting another people's constitution from its related environment and inserting it in the midst of a different society. Nor do certain of Vianna's arguments seem open to refutation. Yet when Vargas overthrew that Constitution and cast around for a method of institutionalizing the dictatorship, his Estado Novo borrowed heavily from the Mussolinian brand of Fascism to which Vianna himself was by no means unsympathetic.

Viewed in the light of such a past, how is the present phase of Brazil's politics to be interpreted? Granted the undeniable fact that the Constitution of 1946 is a second attempt to work in a format taken from the United States, the original questions are still posed—as are also some new ones. For the contemporary Brazilian scene bristles with anomalies. There is the same tussle as previously between a democratizing potential and an entrenched oligarchy. There is the antithesis between an assertive nationalism and the need for outside aid—governmental, as well as economic and social. In addition, until recently, there was the Shavian spectacle of an elderly dictator emeritus, elected peacefully to the presidency of a constitutional régime similar to that which he had formerly subverted. These incongruities can perhaps be best understood in reference to such fundamental topics as federalism, the electorate, the political parties, and the presidency. Together, these illustrate the contradictory character of today's Brazil.

II

The form which federal union has assumed in Brazil is a subject which tempts, but eludes, precise definition. Assuredly the country possesses many attributes which, being associated elsewhere with an authentic brand of federalism, would seem to be its preconditions. Although the huge dimensions which Brazil occupies on the map are illusory, true it is that settlement follows the bulge and length of an extensive coastline, that major centers of population are

separated by considerable distances, and that internal communications are woefully inadequate. From the earliest
days of the Portuguese *capitanias* through the successive
economic cycles of sugar, minerals and precious metals,
and coffee, immigration and development have followed
paths of regional concentration. Variations in climate, soil,
and resources have given rise to divergent interests. Regionalism is a reality that is deeply ingrained in Brazilian
patterns of life, habits of thought and feeling, and political
loyalties. The *gaúcho, paulista, mineiro, carioca,* and *ser-
tanejo* [respectively from Rio Grande do Sul, São Paulo,
Minas Gerais, Rio de Janeiro, and the arid northeast] are
symbols of a historic past and a present consciousness. The
works of literature, art, and scholarship both reproduce
and reinforce the actuality of regionalism. Witnesses to this
are the historical classic of Euclides da Cunha, *Os Sertões,*
and Cândido Portinari's paintings of famine-stricken *ser-
tanejos;* Gilberto Freyre's study of the sociology of the
sugar plantations of Bahia and Pernambuco in *Casa
Grande e Senzala;* Oliveira Vianna's glorification of the
bandeirantes of São Paulo; the picture of metropolitan
sophistication in the novels of Machado de Assis, or the
architecture of Oscar Niemeyer; the *mineiro's* battle to
make the hard rocks yield him wealth and welfare as
chiselled in the tense sculptures of Aleijadinho, "The Little Cripple"; and Érico Veríssimo's romance of the Rio
Grandense frontiersmen re-enacting on the southern pampas the age-old Portuguese determination to push back the
Spaniard.

Centralized government would not seem, in the light of
such facts, to come naturally to Brazil. Yet centralization
was the rule up to 1890, both under the Portuguese and
during the Empire, and it was revived by Vargas between
1930 and 1945. The federalism now officially in force
spells a reaction against the practices of his dictatorship
(particularly its *interventores*) and thereby marks a return,

with modifications, to the ideas of 1890. In the present
Constitution there are features to which a purist who takes
his cue from K. C. Wheare [in *Federal Government*
(1946)] will object on the ground that they tilt the scales
too heavily in the federal government's favor. One example
is the provision, though hedged around with safeguards,
that allows in special circumstances for federal intervention in a state (articles 7–14). Another is the amending
process, which leaves the power of decision and ratification
solely to the National Congress without further reference
to the state legislatures or to popular referendum (article
217).

Federalism is an attempt to provide the constitutional
structure for a political equilibrium. Two prime conditions
must always be met if a federal system is to operate genuinely. First, since formal grants of authority have little
practical effect unless adequately supported by fiscal
means, the distribution of powers among the different levels
of government must be matched by the distribution of
revenues. Second, because a living constitution incorporates
political actualities, and because the latter are shaped
within the context of the surrounding society, it is rash to
assume that a legal document, however skillfully drafted,
can create an equilibrium in a society that is unbalanced.
How do these tests apply to Brazil?

Those who framed the Constitution of 1946 had a clear,
definite intention. They sought to diminish the powers of
the Union and to extend those of the member-states.
Within the latter, too, they wished to strengthen the local
bodies. For these objectives they had sound justification,
both political and social. The result of the policies of
preceding decades had been to accentuate an uneven and
disproportionate development. In the south, as one of Brazil's most eminent economists expressed it to me, the standard of living is comparable to that of central Europe;
whereas in the north and the interior it is about on the

level of most of Asia. The tax system, which Aliomar Baleeiro has so trenchantly analyzed, for many decades favored the interest of the richer individuals and richer regions. The influential landowning oligarchy avoided their fair share of taxation, placing most of the burden on indirect taxes which fell heavily on consumers with small purses. Programs of expenditure improved the amenities of the two great cities of Rio de Janeiro and São Paulo, and, to a lesser degree, of the state capitals elsewhere. But the welfare of the mass of the population, of whom the great majority live on the land, was neglected.

The attempt to correct this disequilibrium is revealed in several provisions of the new Constitution. For example, the most populous states are deliberately under-represented in the National Chamber of Deputies. . . . In the sphere of finance the Constitution explicitly provides that the Union must transfer fixed percentages of the yield of designated taxes on a proportional basis to state and local treasuries (article 15, para. 2, 4). The same precaution is taken to see that the states also will distribute a percentage of certain of their revenues to the local level, and especially to *municípios*[2] other than that containing the capital city (articles 20, 21). Furthermore, the Constitution, which thus accords a status to the *município,* also recognizes the national interest in some regional problems which transcend the resources of the states directly concerned. Singled out for special mention are the problems of the economic development of the Valley of the Amazon and the periodic drought in the arid northeast (articles 198-9). To both of these purposes the federal government—as well as the states and localities of the area—are obliged to devote a minimum amount of their revenue; and in the particular

---

[2] The *município* is the basic unit of local government. It may comprise a city with little or no rural fringe, or a rural area with one or more urban centers, or a large tract of land with a thin and scattered population.

case of the northeast a portion of the federal contribution must be set aside in a reserve fund for relief when disaster strikes.

What has been the effect to date of these well-intentioned conceptions? A part of them, so far, have been imperfectly realized; others, not at all. . . . It is true that the Union's slice of the total tax revenues has diminished somewhat of recent years, though it is the states, rather than the *municípios,* which have been the principal gainers. However, since the Union still absorbs about half the public revenue, it remains financially predominant. Moreover, the direction in which Brazil has moved since 1946 could not fail to enlarge the scope of federal responsibility. Handicapped hitherto by a backward technology and utilizing but a scant amount of its available resources, the country has now plunged at a dizzy speed into grandiose programs of modernization and development: the large-scale financing and construction of basic public works and utilities; control of imports and exports; encouragement of domestic industries; negotiation of foreign loans and technical aid; the influence of monetary policy and the fight against inflation. Such measures, simultaneously undertaken, have prompted an avalanchelike economic momentum. The inescapable political result of this economic development has been an increase in federal power, both because many of the recent programs depended on external policy and assistance and because no state, except São Paulo, possessed the wherewithal to do the job. Even so, despite this far-reaching activity, the federal authorities have not fulfilled some of the obligations which the Constitution makes mandatory. For instance, during the Brazilian summer and fall of 1952–53 the northeast was again stricken by one of the severe and prolonged droughts which recur in its climatic cycle. When the people of the backlands were dying of starvation, or, if they could muster the cash, were fleeing south by the truckload, the federal government organized too little relief that arrived too late for many of the famished victims. It then transpired that the federal government had never yet paid into an emergency fund the annual amounts which the Constitution directed. . . . When this can happen, what force does the Constitution enjoy?

The same question can be applied in yet another sense. So pronounced is the present imbalance in Brazil's social and economic development that constitutional correctives can take effect but slowly and somewhat feebly. In form the Union is composed of 20 states, plus the Federal District, which has virtually the constitutional position of a state, and 4 territories. In substance, however, these states are extremely diverse in population, wealth, and area; and wide is the gap between the living standards of the ten weakest members and the two or three most highly advanced. For all effective purposes modern Brazil consists of its southeastern corner, a rectangular strip about 300 miles wide, running parallel to the coast and stretching from the Uruguayan frontier up to about the 18° of latitude. The north and northeast are depressed, dependent, regions. They may be considered the virtual colonies of the progressive south. As for the interior, most of the area comprised in Amazonas, Mato Grosso, and Pará has never been occupied and settled, and integrated with the coastal strip. Over perhaps two-fifths of its territory the writ of the central government does not run.

The two states with the largest population, São Paulo and Minas Gerais, contain 32.5 percent of the total population according to the census of 1950. From 1890 to 1930 their partnership was the controlling factor in Brazilian government. By gentlemen's agreement, the presidency normally alternated between a *paulista* and a *mineiro*. Jointly the two states furthered their respective economic interests in what Brazilians have called "coffee-and-milk politics" (*política de café com leite*), a reference to the plantations of the one state and the cattle-herds of the other. That alliance, broken by the Vargas *golpe* of 1930, has been hard to re-cement because of the economic and demographic shifts of the last two decades. São Paulo passed Minas in population at the 1940 census and its lead has lengthened ever since. . . .

Meanwhile the city of São Paulo has developed into a mighty metropolis, whose concentration of manufacturing industries is without parallel in present-day Latin America. Like Rio de Janeiro, which it now exceeds in size, São Paulo contains more than 2½ million people. Together, these two cities, holding one-tenth of Brazil's population, contribute the bulk of the manufacturing wealth and tax revenues, and exhibit a technology and living standard dramatically different from those of the rest of the country. . . .

How quickly the federal government can modify these inequalities, and how much it is actually doing to help the weaker regions and spread the benefits of development, is a matter of controversy. There are, of course, plans galore. Brazil luxuriates with plans as the jungle with vegetation. But a paragraph of achievement is always worth a book of promises. What are the accomplished facts which could be the pointers of hope to the future? Various credit items may here be cited. One is the feat of the National Malaria Service, a federal agency, which by systematic spraying with D.D.T. reduced the number of deaths due to malaria, as recorded throughout Brazil, from a total of 31,461 in 1945 to 588 in 1951. Another is the spectacular inauguration at Volta Redonda of the largest iron and steel works in Latin America. Aided in its inception by technicians and capital from the United States, this public enterprise is now supplying about a third of Brazil's expanding requirements. It is located neither in Rio nor São Paulo but between them (though nearer to the former) in a well-planned and newly constructed "government-company town." . . . A third important advance is the construction at Paulo Afonso

on the São Francisco River of a giant dam, which supplies
hydroelectric energy to Bahia and Pernambuco. Fourth is
the inauguration in Bahia of an oil refinery and smallish
oil field, and the recent discovery of oil in the Amazon
Valley. Fifth is the attempt to encourage settlement in the
interior by developing the plateau of Goiás which between 1940 and 1950 was the second-fastest state in growth.
Lastly there is the slowly maturing labor of conciliating the
Chavante Indians, a task so notably inspired by General
Rondon. These and similar changes constitute an impressive list. They signalize a definite progress. They must,
however, be augmented manyfold before Brazil will be
"over the hump" and its contrasts reduced to less glaring
proportions.

III

If other aspects of the governmental process—such as
the parties, electorate, presidency, and Congress—are
studied, the same struggle reappears between form and substance, between innovation and tradition, between a political concept on the one hand and the economic and social
context on the other. If Brazil is to become the representative democracy, which the Constitution affirms, two requirements at least are clearly implied. The people, from
whom all power is declared to emanate (article 1), must
be all-inclusive, and they and their representatives must be
organized in the kind of party system that can give their
politics direction, cohesion, and purpose. How far has
Brazil progressed in applying these ideas?

In its favor a fact of great importance is its racial policy.
Since Brazilians derive from 3 distinct racial stocks—
American Indian, African Negro, and European Caucasian
—mixed or unmixed, the attitude that prevails nationally
on matters of race and color has a vital bearing on the
future prospects of democracy. Judged in this light, Brazil

is seen at its best. For its size and heterogeneity the country probably exhibits less discrimination based upon race,
more positive acceptance of interracial marriages, and
therefore more hope for the future, than any comparable
case. Now this does not mean that in the differences which
so acutely divide Brazilian society, namely inequalities of
social class and wealth, the factor of race is irrelevant.
Far from it. One can demonstrate indisputably that as a
general rule the higher the bracket of wealth, social status,
education, and living standards, the lighter is the color of
the skin. That most of the privileged people are the
whitest and that most of the darkest are underprivileged
is a fact. But it must be noted that these distinctions are
not grounded in, or justified by, a doctrine of racism. The
notion that one race is inherently superior to another does
not gain credence in Brazil and only aroused a furious
reaction when the Nazis sought to propagate it. The bar-
riers that divide human beings in Brazil are in the main
social and economic, not racial. Since democratic politics
require the equal treatment of everybody in fundamentals,
Brazil's wise handling of its racial relations offers an augury
of further democratization.

Hitherto, however, the country has not experienced a
system of government under which the majority of the
adult population can participate in the choice of its rulers.
If Brazil today be compared with the fully developed
democracies, it evidently still has a long way to go. Compared with its own past, however, it has already traveled
some distance. Thus, in 1933, less than 1½ million were
registered as voters. At the presidential elections of 1950
that figure had risen to 11,600 thousand; in the congres-
sional contest of October 1954, it reached 15,500 thousand. Even when allowance is made for increase in population, this marks a significant extension for a 21-year
period. But there are many millions who are still denied
the suffrage. In 1950 . . . the registered electorate . . .

was only 42 percent of those above the minimum age. The disfranchisement of the remaining 58 percent was due, in large part, to the constitutional requirement that in order to vote a citizen must be literate. The census of 1950 disclosed that literates numbered 42.7 percent of those over the age of five; and the percentage of literates among those eighteen and over may be assumed to have been rather smaller.

Under the present Constitution, therefore, a fuller approximation to democracy depends on the spread of education. But, unfortunately, the rate of progress in this vital field does not match the rapidity with which industrialization is being pushed. Literates were 38.5 percent of the population in 1940, and 42.7 percent in 1950. A gain of 4.2 percent, however, is far from adequate to conquer illiteracy in the early future. Getúlio Vargas was not as great an educator as he was an industrializer. Nor, indeed, is it possible after a sojourn in Brazil to avoid the belief that, while many states and localities lack the money to educate the masses, some of the country's leading citizens also lack the wish. . . .

This attitude towards the common people is further reflected in the nature of the political parties. Prior to 1930, the kernel of party organization lay in the states. National politics were controlled by interstate coalitions, rather than by the growth of a party structure at the center. Vargas centralized the system in the thirties, trying to obliterate the state movements and to create a single national party loyal to himself. As the opponents of his régime gathered strength, they too combined in a central movement with the same União Democrática Nacional (U.D.N.) indicating that they were not a party but a union. With the opportunities for free political association which the end of the dictatorship provided, parties speedily proliferated in a manner that was wondrous to behold. Because they were so numerous, they placed in the Constitution a clause requiring "the system of proportional representation" (article 56) in the elections of the Câmara, which is the more potent of the two houses. . . .

In the Câmara chosen in 1950, 11 parties held 229 of the 304 seats, the other 75 members having been elected by two or more parties in various combinations. For the most part Brazilian parties continue to be state organizations. But in a few cases there are central structures, varying in cohesiveness. Only 4 parties possess national significance. The Partido Social Democrático (P.S.D.), which holds nearly a third of the seats of the Câmara, was the "official" party of the Dutra period. It thus contains many persons who then secured position and preferment. The U.D.N., ranking second, is a mixture of the conservative right and of some highly educated professional men. It includes an aristocracy of talent that is qualitatively important but devoid of a mass base. Third comes the Partido Trabalhista Brasileiro (P.T.B.) which was Vargas' post-war creation. It is nationalistic, friendly to industrialism, and sympathetic to urban labor. Fourth is the Partido Social Progressista (P.S.P.), led by Adhemar de Barros, with its strength concentrated in São Paulo of which state he was formerly governor. It has one program: to elect "Adhemar" to the presidency. The Communist Party, whose strength was increasing in the first post-war elections, was outlawed in 1947. It is still very active, but its exact strength cannot be gauged.

That the parties severally are immature, that too many sprang up too soon, and that the system as a whole is precarious seems scarcely open to question. Under the forms of a multi-party organization the realities of oligarchy continue with little abatement. There are various ways in which the machinery lends itself to the manipulations of a few. For example, Brazil has not yet adopted a ballot that is printed and distributed by the state and contains the names of all candidates. Instead, ballots are printed, at their own expense, by the parties and the candidates for a particular office, without including, of course, the names of the opponents. So if you wish to vote for Senhor X as your deputy, you must obtain a ballot with his name printed on it, which you place in the box on election day. Should you want to split your ticket by voting for candidates of different parties for the various offices, you must secure a ballot from each candidate, a chore that may put some strain on the conscientiousness of the independent citizen.

For their part, the candidates are required to meet some formidable expenditures. The printing of ballots is itself a large item. One deputy explained to me that he had distributed 200 thousand ballots in order to fetch a yield of 11 thousand actual votes. Many voters solicit the candidate for gifts of clothing or cash. Since each constituency is an entire state, or a large metropolis like Rio, a candidate must campaign extensively and the traveling costs him money. In addition, he pays for his own advertising prior to the election. Then on the fateful day he is expected to bring voters to the polls in cars which in many places are difficult to obtain, and he should offer them a lunch for their trouble. . . .

To enter politics in Brazil, therefore, a man must have wealth or wealthy friends. Yet it is not in order to make money that he becomes a member of Congress. Indeed, his seat there may cause him some loss of capital. What he does expect to gain is power and prestige. He wishes to protect his interests, to preserve his local position, by exercising control over legislation and by bargaining with the government. Thus the adoption of a constitution written in the language of democracy has not resulted, at least immediately, in the elimination of oligarchy. What has altered is the machinery, or the external procedures, which it is necessary for the oligarchy to employ in order to keep on the top of the heap. In most of the rural areas, quasi-feudal in their social structure and therefore conservative in attitude, the maintenance by the few of their privileged position has not hitherto proved too difficult. While only 3 percent of Brazil's land is put to agricultural use, ownership is concentrated in *latifundia*. The Minister of Agriculture, João Cleophas, stated to a session of the United Nations Commission for Latin America in 1953 that 7.8 percent of the landowners (those whose holdings exceeded 200 hectares) possessed 73 percent of the land. Plans have been discussed to compel the big landholders to sell whatever land they do not put to productive use. But there appears to be no disposition to hurry with a scheme that has the makings of an agrarian revolution. In the meantime the social and economic predominance of a rural oligarchy is transferred to politics in the form of the *coronel,* or boss, who may be one of the big *fazendeiros* himself or else closely associated with their interests. . . .

Similarly in urban areas the elections, because of their costliness, are generally controlled by oligarchical influences. But it is possible in the cities for a popular upheaval to occur in exceptional cases. That was what happened in March 1953, in Brazil's most advanced metropolis, São Paulo. The election was a local one to fill the office of *prefeito* (mayor); but the results had the same national significance as, say, an election in the United States for the mayoralty of New York City. At that time Brazil's chronic inflation was mounting, sharply and dangerously, like a fever. The rise in prices depressed the real wages of urban workers. Economic discontent found its outlet in a dramatic political overturn. Four candidates ran, of whom the favorite had the support of the 3 major political parties plus the backing of the former Governor, Adhemar de Barros. He lost, however, to an opponent who, though he represented only a minor party, polled two-thirds of the total vote. The victor, Jânio Quadros, was described by the losing side as a demagogue. But whether that name was merited or not, it was he at that moment who responded to a sorely felt social need. . . .

Such episodes do more than reveal the factions that "war within the bosom of a single state." They also indicate the point to which politics have evolved in present-day Brazil. The parties are as the foam on the breaking surf. But the wave is impelled by currents that lie deeper. In Brazil, whatever the outward forms, the dynamics of political movement are still provided by two traditional forces. One of these is the activity of pressure groups. Contemporary Brazil has pressure-group politics, but not party politics. Pressure groups—in the sense either of potent institutions or of organized interests—are highly influential in shaping the policies which the government espouses. Political periods and presidents resemble, or differ from, one another according to which groups expect and receive prior consideration. Apart from the church and the army, which few politicians dare openly to oppose, the principal pressure groups are economic. Under the Empire the sugar interest of the northeast was the major one. With the establishment of the Republic, São Paulo coffee producers, allied to Minas Gerais, took the leadership from Pernambuco and Bahia. Vargas held power and, after the Dutra interregnum, regained it by enlisting on his side the newer industrial and urban proletariat. His régime tended to help the manufacturers and importers; while exporting interests, like the coffee kings, complained of discrimination. The labor code, the social-security system, and the mercantilist program have all been designed from a mixture of nationalist, political, and economic motives. The industrial employees, unionized in corporative fashion and bureaucratically managed by the Ministry of Labor, received the benefits of a paternalistic security which they lacked before. They responded with loyalty to "Getúlio" during the dictatorship, by voting for him in 1950, and by mourning and riots upon his demise.

Of the traditional forces which continue to energize Brazilian politics, the second, as the preceding paragraph implies, is the leadership of an individual personality. Many of the pressures generated within the economic and social systems are canalized by a single person for the reason that to most Brazilians government is not comprehensible except in terms of one man. The monarchical symbol represented by the House of Braganza was continued under the Empire in the distinguished and respected figure of Dom Pedro II. Brazil thus differed from the United States in separating the acts of achieving independence and republicanism by almost seven decades. Since 1890 one unbroken institutional thread uniting modern Brazil with its past has been the presidency. Not only does the office represent psychologically the Brazilian familiarity with the preeminence of one individual, but it also transfers to politics the structure characteristic of the family, school, and church. Hence some "parties" are simply the shadow cast by a man, as, nationally, the P.T.B. stood to Vargas or the P.S.P. to de Barros, or, locally, they are so weak as to break before a popular tide drawn by the pull of a Jânio Quadros. For the rest, these parties are minority groupings of politicians, many of them individually of high caliber, but necessarily weak since their roots are not in the mass of the populace.

If the meaningful party system, simplified in structure and democratic in spirit, is to triumph over pressure groups and *personalismo,* other institutions as well as the state must undergo change. The reform of Brazilian politics is still hampered not only by a high rate of illiteracy, but by some persistent attributes of the family system and the church. Certain great families (or clans) continue to fill a disproportionately large number of the high offices of state. Behind the forms of government there lie the informal connections that unite officials by bonds of kinship. Such relationships delay the task of achieving a broader conception of the public interest and of civic responsibility. Likewise, the church cannot be counted as a force for progress. Though traditionally less potent in Brazil than in many countries of Latin America, ecclesiastical influence on attitudes and conduct can scarcely be ignored. The somewhat static conservatism that marks its leadership does not aid the efforts of constitutional innovators. Moreover, its rural predilections are scarcely well-adapted to the contemporary growth of industry. For the state to grapple with the dynamic disturbances of the economy would be in any case difficult. But difficulties are certainly accentuated when political improvement is in part dependent on changes in other institutions of society which take place much more slowly.

IV

The government of Brazil resembles an airplane winging its way over mountain peaks while [an] economic blizzard rocks the craft and lashes the people below. Economic stringency impels the São Paulo populace to use a local election to register their protest against national misplanning, although the *prefeito* of a city has not the powers to check a national inflation. . . . Climatic rigors and chronic poverty drive the *nordestinos* to premature death or to the greener south. And though the Constitution prescribes for their misfortunes, their widespread illiteracy— an index to their social retardation—nullifies the political force they can exert. Rapid industrialization brings into political focus the needs of an urbanized, wage-earning public. But the concentration of wealth and amassing of vast fortunes (that of the Matarazzos being the extreme case) intensifies the power of oligarchy. Meanwhile, an absence of political idealism has its counterpart in the mood of the skeptical and the disillusioned, and leaves a vacuum of morale.

Into a vacuum any winds can blow. Because Brazil is passing through its industrial revolution before it has achieved a constitutional consensus, what course its politics will take is anybody's guess. Great danger lies in the fact that no political *modus vivendi* has yet been reached for bridging the gap between social statics and economic dynamics. Hence the present stage of Brazilian politics is pre-revolutionary. The fissionable material now accumulating, however, could be detonated in any one of various explosions. There is the real possibility that the democratic concept, now existing largely on paper, may develop increasingly in practice. The signs that point in that direction are: the mature and tolerant policy on racial relations; the vivid intelligence of the best-educated Brazilians; the faculty for self-criticism that is revealed in conversation and the press; and, the balance and proportion that come from possessing a sense of humor. But frustration, injustice, authoritarianism, and insecurity can just as surely be the precursors of Communism or Fascism, or something akin to Peronism. Meanwhile, the national motto of "Order and Progress" defines an ideal rather than describes the facts. Many changes are occurring, but not all change is synonymous with progress; and it is hard to say whether order or disorder is currently the more prominent. Amid these uncertainties only one thing is sure. Since it is the function of the state to be the equilibrator of society, the supreme challenge for Brazil in the mid-twentieth century is to achieve its own political renaissance from within.

✦§20§✦

Timothy F. Harding

Revolution Tomorrow: The Failure of the Left

The Brazilian crisis finally came to a head in the coup d'état of 1964, which threw out the already mangled Constitution of 1946. Since much had been said to suggest that Brazil was on the verge of a communist revolution led by the President himself, many were surprised by the ease with which he was overthrown. Professor Timothy F. Harding of California State College at Los Angeles here argues that Brazil was not in that position: not only was the President precariously balanced in the center, but the forces that conceivably would have pushed him leftward were divided and weak. The article below appeared only a few months after the events it analyzed and was perhaps the first to deal seriously with the coup d'état. It reveals Professor Harding's familiarity with the Brazilian political scene and its labor history.

From Timothy F. Harding, "Revolution Tomorrow: The Failure of the Left in Brazil," *Studies on the Left*, IV, No. 4 (Fall 1964), 30–55. This selection is from pp. 30–39, 41, 43–44, 46–52. Reprinted by permission of the publisher.

The rightist coup that toppled the regime of Brazilian President João Goulart in April [1964] ended the "institutionalized crisis" that had plagued the government since the resignation of Jânio Quadros in August 1961. The coup upset the intricate balance among labor, bureaucracy, landowners, and commercial and industrial interests which had characterized Brazilian politics since Getúlio Vargas took power in the Revolution of 1930. The Goulart government was trying to maintain leadership of revolutionary forces in Brazilian society while clinging to the wealthy conservative power elite. The new government has set out to destroy the power of the Brazilian labor movement, so carefully nurtured since 1930 as an ally of the government.

What led the military to overthrow Goulart's centrist government? What are the leftist forces in Brazil; what kind of leadership do they have; why were they unable to head off a right-wing coup? What prospects does the Brazilian left have under the new dictatorial regime?

[*Historical Background and the Rise of Labor*]

The Goulart Regime was an extension of the political alliance forged by Getúlio Vargas in 1930. . . . During the world depression decade, Vargas constructed a viable political system based on young army officers (the jacobin "tenentes"), budding urban industrialists—industry expanded during the depression and World War II, when Brazil's ability to import consumer goods was reduced— a labor movement created and controlled by the Labor Ministry, and a swollen middle-class government bureaucracy. Government intervention in the economy increased, culminating, during World War II, in the national steel plant at Volta Redonda. However, Vargas, a large landholder in his native state of Rio Grande do Sul, did not disturb the agricultural sector, and soon incorporated the landholding class, increasingly inseparable from the commercial and industrial sector, into his political system. Coffee and sugar plantations became dependent upon government purchase of excess production.

Above all, the Vargas system was designed to avoid class conflict by making the state arbiter between capital and labor. A government-controlled labor movement was constructed and workers were given a paternalistic labor code and a vast social-welfare program which remained largely on paper until unions became strong enough to demand enforcement. At first the government supported official labor leaders in obtaining recognition and concessions from employers. During the Estado Novo (1937–45) Vargas set up a corporativist dictatorship under which strikes were outlawed. Unions became organs of government at the mercy of the Labor Ministry.

The advent of "democracy" and a liberal constitution in 1945 did not free labor from official control, for the corporativist organization of labor and management and the government machinery to mediate remained intact. Serious wage conflicts continued to be resolved by government intervention. If a union did not accept the government's decision, it was breaking the law and its conflict was with the government, not with the employer. Labor organizations were, and are still, financially controlled by the Labor Ministry through the union tax, one day's salary a year from every worker in a given sector, union member or not, that is collected by the government and turned over to the union to supplement dues. Only a small percentage of workers in most labor sectors belong to the union, but the union-negotiated wage agreements apply to non-members as well. Moreover, the Ministry can disavow union elections if it dislikes the results, and can name interventors.

However, after 1945 the government buffer between capital and labor wore thin, labor relations deteriorated, and strikes became more frequent. The mechanism of labor control tended to shift from the Ministry to the political party. Gradually, a more independent labor leadership emerged demanding ever-greater concessions in return for political support. . . .

Although politically the Kubitschek government [1955–1960] maintained a neutral position between capital and labor, the economic policy of inflation . . . worked to the disadvantage of those who lived on salaries. The government, and particularly labor-boss and Vice President Goulart, seemed to support unions' demands, allowing agitation, and guaranteeing sizeable wage increases to unions with militant labor leadership, but the net effect was only a partial recovery once a year of the loss caused by the erosion of real wages. Labor leadership expended its efforts to regain income lost through inflation, a conservative aim accompanied by radical methods.

Inflation did not produce social upheaval immediately because the real growth of the economy during the Kubitschek period brought upward mobility. Many ambitious workers acquired skills that brought higher salaries. While average wages rose more slowly than prices, the demand for skilled labor in São Paulo pulled up wages in some categories faster than the cost of living. Rural workers poured into the cities; some peasants and slum-dwellers entered the ranks of "labor." They experienced immediate improvement by their change of class and thus remained satisfied for a time, even if inflation watered down their new wages. Family income often increased when wives and daughters went to work in industry and commerce; before, only males had regularly sought such employment. Minimum wages were raised by government decree often enough to keep down agitation. With government arbitration of wage disputes and ministry control of some union leadership, it was possible to keep labor begging for favors from the government. . . .

The most important political forces in the labor movement after 1945 were the Communist Party and the PTB.

Under [Eurico Gaspar] Dutra's Presidency (1946–50) the Communists were outlawed (partly because they did so well in the 1945 and 1947 elections), and many Communist leaders were hounded out of the labor movement. Though still illegal, they re-entered labor with Vargas' election in 1950. While they were initially hostile to Vargas and Goulart, after Vargas' suicide in 1954 the Communists began to work with the PTB and the PSD in opposition to right-wing elements in the Army and the UDN. In 1956 they dropped their opposition to the "union tax" since, as an important part of the labor leadership, they were benefiting from it. The PTB allowed the Communists to run some candidates under PTB labels. In return the Communist Party provided disciplined cadres which the PTB sorely needed. Goulart and the PTB controlled the distribution of government jobs in labor courts and social security institutes. These jobs made it possible for labor leaders to live in the middle class, from which a great many had come. The support of the Communist and PTB labor leaders helped Kubitschek maintain the Vargas alliance between labor, middle class, and industrialist, as well as landowners, to the end of his presidency in 1960.

In the absence of cohesive political parties with ideology, nationalism became the most important political movement in Brazil, particularly after Vargas' suicide. The nationalist movement helped hold together the alliance between labor, middle class, and some industrialists. Vargas had exploited economic nationalism to win support: Petrobrás, the national oil company created in 1953, became the leading symbol of the movement. Vargas' suicide note intensified nationalist indignation. Kubitschek added the symbol of Brasília; during his regime nationalism was built into a loosely-organized movement, financed by the government and national business interests that feared foreign competition. Nationalist activists included unscrupulous politicians seeking fast profit, often with investments in land, industry, and urban real estate, students, elements in the military, and the Communist Party. The movement was whipped up into a feverish anti-imperialist campaign that blamed all Brazilian ills on exploitation by foreign "trusts." Nationalism provided political support for Kubitschek's "developmentism" and channeled all potentially revolutionary activity into unproductive demonstrations against imperialism. . . .

Quadros' election [in 1960] was a repudiation of the demagogic middle-class nationalistic movement officially utilized in support of Lott. The Brazilian worker and mid-but had become aware that the nationalist movement was being used as an escape valve for social discontent by national employers who were paying lower wages and making higher profit rates than foreign companies. . . . Quadros' unwillingness and inability to mobilize mass support against his enemies resulted in his isolation and resignation or deposition. . . . In view of Quadros' failure, Goulart, discredited and linked with corruption and the status quo, had little chance of passing any basic reforms. Brazilians were again saddled with what they had elected Quadros to replace. . . .

The Forces of the Left: The Communist Parties

To understand the failure of the left to stave off a rightist coup and the prospects for revolution in the future we must examine leftist leadership in Brazil.

The Communist Party split in late 1961, ostensibly over the Sino-Soviet dispute but equally over the Cuban Revolution. The pro-Moscow group led by Luís Carlos Prestes, a man with considerable popular prestige, is known as the Partido Comunista Brasileiro (PCB). The pro-Chinese group took the name Partido Comunista do Brasil (PC do B). After the split the PCB continued to take a very moderate reformist line, accusing more radical groups of adventurism. Prestes' group insisted that there were no objective conditions for revolution in Brazil, and that basic reforms could be achieved by supporting Goulart and pushing him to the left. In general the PCB proclaimed its aim to be the destruction of feudalism and imperialism. This would be achieved through alliance with the "progressive bourgeoisie" and the achievement of a "democratic and popular" government such as the Goulart regime to which they gave "critical" support.

The PC do B was formed by a group led by João Amazonas, Pedro Pomar, and Maurício Gabrois, who had all been downgraded in the old party for being "Stalinists" after the Twentieth Congress of the Soviet Communist Party. The PC do B leaders took advantage of the Sino-Soviet split and the dissatisfaction over the party's conservative position on the part of much of the Communist youth and some militant labor cadres, particularly in Niteroi (state of Rio de Janeiro). These militants felt that the Communist line of support for the "progressive bourgeoisie" had been discredited by the success of the Cuban Revolution. The Communist militants were attracted by the Chinese position on pushing revolution in underdeveloped countries. However, the PC do B had trouble keeping its student support, since a young person attracted by the Cuban Revolution was reluctant to accept the old-time leadership of those who admired the Peking regime because of the Chinese defense of Stalinism!

The CGT

Independent of the Communists and working with both factions, there emerged from the PTB labor leaders involved in the CGT [General Confederation of Labor], a group that was radical, independent, and leftist, although somewhat discredited by its opportunistic past and the

corruption which has tinged nearly all labor leaders that
rose above the rank of factory delegate. This group, including some railroad-union leaders, came from the ranks
of the PTB but received their syndical and political education from the PCB before the party split. The Communist
schism and Goulart's loss of control of labor gave this
group a chance to make their voices felt through the
CGT. They went underground during the coup and are one
potential rallying point for future revolutionary leadership. . . .

Peasant Movements

The leaderships of the various peasant movements in
Brazil are another rallying point for revolution. The peasant only began to be a political force after 1959 when
Francisco Julião reached national—and later international
—fame as leader of the "Peasant Leagues" of the Northeast. Most peasants could not vote because they were illiterate. Most of those that could vote supported conservative
candidates at the bidding of their land-owning boss. . . .

While from an economic point of view Brazilian agriculture is more capitalist than feudal, the social system in
agriculture is one of extreme paternalism, more so in the
Northeast than in the center-south. The word paternalism
connotes the benevolent side of a relationship between
landowner and peasant that has had as its complement
violence and cruelty when the peasant dared demand rights
or improvement of his condition. The advent of effective
peasant leadership was delayed by the ability of the landowner to crush insubordination with violence which rarely
came to the attention of urban Brazil. . . .

From 1930 on, the gap between rural and urban Brazil
widened. Rural workers were prohibited from organizing
unions and were denied social security and protective labor
legislation. Inflation isolated the peasant from the national

market. The breakdown of rural paternalism proceeded at a slower rate than the development of urban class consciousness and "mass society."

Combative peasant organizations appeared, not in the vital coffee, cacao, sugar, and cattle sectors, but where paternalism had broken down and the conflict was most intense between peasant and landowner: in marginal *fazendas* that were hard-pressed to compete with more modernized commercial sectors of agriculture; and in frontier areas and land near cities where, because of the rise in land value, speculators and commercial farmers were moving in to grab land from squatters who had cleared and farmed the land.

The former was the case in the Northeast where Francisco Julião, a lawyer and deputy in the Pernambuco state assembly, gave urban political leadership to a group of peasants on a property called *Galilea* (Galilee) located in the transitional area (*agreste*) between the wet coastal sugar lands and the arid cattle properties to the west. Galilea, a marginal mandioca and vegetable fazenda, had once grown sugar on its impoverished soils. The owner brought about the organization of the first league when he tried to expel the peasants so that he could "modernize" his property by converting it to cattle. While the peasants at Galilea defended themselves from the landowner's violence, Julião fought their case in court and pressured the Pernambuco State Governor into expropriating the property. It became a cooperative.

With this success, which took four years (1955–59), the Leagues spread in Pernambuco and Paraíba, but they generally stayed west of the populous coastal sugar lands. They were fought by local landowners with bullets and clubs. They provided, for the first time, an opportunity for the violence of the rural landowner to be brought to the attention of the urban public and for rural conflicts to be resolved in the urban political environment.

Before Julião, the Left in Brazil had attracted no effective peasant support in the Northeast. Rural politicians were usually landowners or their servants and unwilling to stir up the peasantry. Urban politicians were not interested in illiterates who had no vote. Leftists looked to the working class rather than the peasantry as the motive force of social change. In addition, urban politicians did not know how to communicate with the peasant. Julião, like Fidel Castro the son of a landowner, developed his natural ability to communicate with agricultural workers. In an area which has abounded in religious fanatics who have developed powerful mystical movements, Julião preached in parables of Communist China and Cuba, of Mao, Fidel, and Jesus Christ. This mystical approach inspired love. Ballad singers spread the story of the Leagues in traditional melody and rhyme.

While the aim of each local branch of the Leagues was to defend the peasant and improve his lot, the aim of Julião's whole movement with its coordinating office in Recife was to politicize the peasant and force the enactment of radical agrarian reform. Julião at first favored peaceful means, but later warned that a revolution would be necessary to achieve meaningful reform. Without the right to vote or organize (the Leagues were registered as civil associations but they did not have labor union status or privileges) and without government intervention to help them, peasants used the Leagues for legal defense and for organizing agitation.

Julião was soon rivaled in promoting peasant organization in the Northeast by a small group of radical Catholic priests including Father Antônio Mello, of Cabo, Pernambuco. In Bahia and Rio Grande do Norte states other priests organized agricultural workers' unions which were eventually legally recognized. These priests used radical rhetoric, and they were fought as subversives by local land-

owners, but their aim was not the destruction of large private land-holdings but "some sort of new deal parity
between the peasant and the latifundist." They wanted technical aid, the right to organize, and better conditions for
the peasant. . . .

These dynamic peasant organizations, based as they were
on marginal rather than primary agriculture, raised the
militant cry of "land for those that till it" and "land reform
or death" since they were clearly involved in mortal struggles over the possession and occupancy of land. There is
no question that the appearance of these organizations
transformed the political consciousness, hopes, and goals
of the most underprivileged segment in Brazilian society.
The revolutionary potential of these Peasant Leagues
should not be under-emphasized just because they do not
base their power on the most economically crucial sectors
of Brazilian agriculture. In Cuba it was the wretched
Oriente peasants, not the rural-proletarian sugar workers,
who first nurtured Fidel's army.

On the other hand, it is not surprising that such organizations would have little appeal to workers in coffee, sugar,
and cacao, whose immediate demand is not land, but higher
income, better housing, and the right to organize. This is
not to say that after a socialist revolution these rural
workers would oppose cooperatives or collectives. However, under present conditions their demands are more
trade-unionist.

The conflict between union-type demands and land demands was in evidence at the first national meeting of
peasant organizations in Belo Horizonte, Minas Gerais, in
November 1961. The presence of political dignitaries was
a sign that peasants had finally arrived on the national
political scene, because of their revolutionary potential.
Julião emerged as the national peasant leader, not only
because of his spectacular role in the Northeast, but be-

cause of his backing from the most radical urban elements, particularly students. The majority of the peasant delegates at the meeting supported Julião's radical position calling for immediate expropriation of large properties. At the conservative pole during the conclave was the Communist Party (PCB) in the form of the leadership of a São Paulo rural workers' organization known as the União dos Lavradores e Trabalhadores Agricolas do Brasil (ULTAB), a trade-union-type group which is older than the Peasant Leagues and has branches among sharecroppers in coffee and some sugar workers in São Paulo state. Although not legally recognized as unions, ULTAB organizations tended to engage in collective bargaining. At the meeting, the ULTAB leaders pushed for elaborate resolutions extending urban labor legislation and protection to workers in the countryside. Their position was unpopular, but they represented, not just the reformist moderacy of the Communist Party in Brazil, but also the trade-union-type demands of the major sectors of Brazilian agriculture which had not been reached by the Leagues.

After the Belo Horizonte meeting the peasant movement rapidly reached its peak and began to decline. The threat to send thousands of peasants to camp on the steps of Congress until the passage of an agrarian reform bill was never carried out. In 1962, Julião was elected as a deputy to the national congress, where he scarcely appeared and hardly ever spoke. He began to be criticized by other leftist elements and declined as a national figure.

There were several reasons for the apparent decline on the national scene (though not locally) of the radical peasant organizations. Julião's leadership kept promising revolution but no revolution came or was organized. Eventually, though the leagues continued to spread, they were no longer news, except in cases of local violence. Secondly, the government, under Goulart, passed (in March, 1963) the law giving rural workers most of the same rights as urban workers, including the right to organize unions. As Caio Prado Junior pointed out, this law was of momentous importance, although most leftist forces ignored it, for by a legal stroke it brought the peasant within the political framework of the nation. This process was completed when Goulart gave illiterates the vote [never enacted into law]. The rural labor law was passed as an attempt to head off peasant agitation, but it gave the peasant the right to demand government intervention to protect him against the landowner. Catholic organizations immediately increased their efforts to organize legal peasant unions and outflank Julião, particularly in the Northeast.

Another reason for Julião and the Leagues' decline was the rise of Miguel Arraes, elected PTB governor of Pernambuco in 1962. Arraes' election was particularly significant because he defeated, with PTB and Communist backing, a candidate who had the support and financial backing of conservative forces from all over Brazil as well as support from the United States in the form of Alliance aid. In Arraes' victory, urban radicalism triumphed over rural conservatism in one of Brazil's most backward states. As governor he took advantage of the rural labor legislation to encourage unionization of sugar workers. With his support, these unions won spectacular wage increases for sugar-mill and field workers, giving a considerable boost to commerce in the interior of Pernambuco and creating a new market for manufactures. The success of Arraes diminished the political status of Julião, and the presence in his own state of a governor friendly to peasant organization reduced Julião's value as a political agitator. Moreover, Julião temporarily isolated himself in 1963 from the rest of the Brazilian Left when he tried to form his own leftist movement, the Movimento Revolucionário Tiradentes (MRT), built on the Peasant Leagues. The MRT alienated labor and student leftists it was designed to attract. Julião was criticized for superficiality, vagueness on the question of agrarian reform, making false promises of "revolution tomorrow," and above all for excessive mysticism (perhaps his most important asset in organizing peasants in the Northeast). Immediately after the coup Julião disappeared, but he was later found disguised as a peasant and imprisoned.

Students

Brazilian student radicals, part of the middle class, have been the most radical element in Brazilian society in that they have been least willing to accept the stagnation and conservatism built into Brazilian government and politics. They believe that the techniques for rapid development of their country exist, the analysis of what is wrong has been made, and yet the mechanisms of politics and government that should transmit the need, desire, and urgency of change, work instead to impede it. They feel an acute responsibility to make a revolution for the rest of the population, as if their tenuous title to the role of intellectual made them the brains of the masses. The freedom from commitment to the status quo stemming from their student status makes them intensely aware of the injustices of society and willing to act to end them. They see themselves as a revolutionary vanguard. These delusions of grandeur are combined with a romantic idea of revolutionary politics. Student meetings are filled with exaggerated posing and self-admiration. Student conferences are elaborately staged, and, if someone plays a scene of agitation until he loses control of himself, the audience applauds the "pretty performance."

The surprising thing, then, is that among student revolutionaries there is a real commitment to improving society as evidenced by the cultural and educational activities of the União Nacional dos Estudantes (UNE—National Student Union). One finds among these students some of the most well-informed and realistic militants of the Brazilian Left.

The UNE has been controlled for years by a coalition between Communists and Acção Popular (AP), a left-wing Catholic young group. AP's humanistic leftist position, the most radical of any Christian Democrat movement in Latin America, was encouraged by Christian Democrat Paulo de Tarso and the small group of priests that work with peasants and slum dwellers.

In third place in the student movement is an independent, Marxist, revolutionary group known as *Política Operária*. This small group was formed in 1961 by radical youth from the PTB, the Brazilian Socialist Party, and the Communist Party, as well as independent Marxists. Pinning their hopes on the radicalization of the labor movement, they made no concessions to expediency and were unrelenting in their attacks on Goulart and the myth that he could effect basic reforms. This estranged them from the PTB, the PCB, and many left-wing nationalists. On the other hand, they were not taken seriously by the dogmatic PC do B or by Julião's MRT. Nevertheless, their influence far outweighed their numbers because of their intellectual qualifications, their integrity, and their "Fidelismo."

The closest thing to a union of leftist forces was achieved a few months before the coup by the Frente de Mobilização Popular (FMP). This was the successor to a series of national liberation movements which discredited politicians had controlled. But the FMP, with Brizola and the CGT labor command in the lead, was certainly the most radical of these fronts. It included all the major radical tendencies: labor, peasants, students, PCB, PC do B, left-wing of the PTB, the Brazilian Socialist Party, and the radical Christian Democrats. However, the fracturing of the Left between demagogues and dedicated leaders, urban and rural masses, middle-class radicals and workers, Northeast and Central-south, and finally between reformists and revolutionaries—all these divisions prevented the mobilization of effective opposition to the rightist coup.

◄§ 21 §►

Helder Pessoa Câmara
and Others

————◄●►————

Bishops and Workers

*It was once the usual practice to link the Catholic
Church in Latin America with the landowners and
the army in a vast conservative conspiracy. The situation was probably never that simple, and it certainly
is not so today; for although many church leaders
are indeed found on the side of the past, many others
look hopefully toward a new and more just future.
One of these is the Archbishop of Olinda and Recife,
Dom Helder Câmara. Said to be one of the important
behind-the-scenes figures at the Second Ecumenical
Council, he has a long-established record for social
concern in Brazil. The statement below—which bears
the imprint of his thought although signed by thirteen bishops—caused a furor when it was issued in
July 1966. The commander of the Fourth Army
based in Recife refused to allow its publication. A
confrontation between the civil and religious powers
seemed imminent until President Castelo Branco flew
from the capital to deal personally with the crisis:*

Translated and printed from *Os bispos do Nordeste II* (*Alagôas,
Pernambuco, Paraíba e Rio Grande do Norte*) *e a situação dos
trabalhadores urbanos e rurais nordestinos,* leaflet (Recife: July 14,
1966), by permission of Dom Helder Câmara.

the army commander was transferred. The translation
given here is from a handbill distributed at that time.
The incident tells us as much about the condition of
Brazil as about the attitude of the bishops.

The bishops of the Second Northeast Region (Alagôas,
Pernambuco, Paraíba, and Rio Grande do Norte), meeting
in regular session[1] on July 12, 13, and 14 [1966] took cog-
nizance of the manifesto of Workers' Catholic Action on
the condition of workers in the northeast and of the report
presented by Rural Catholic Action and by Agrarian
Catholic Youth on the state of affairs in the rural northeast.
With such objective documents before us, we must thank
you, dear militants and assistants, for the contribution that
they make toward truth and justice.

At this meeting we wish to reaffirm our complete solidarity with the workers, especially those who are hungry,
endure oppression, or are the victims of injustice. We
proclaim—with the [Ecumenical] Council—that labor exceeds in value and dignity the other elements of economic
life. We recognize that there cannot be development or
advancement where man is not put in first place. Where the
human person is not respected, where eyes are not turned
to the common welfare, or where the essential equality of
all men is not defended, there cannot be development or
Christianity. Now, the documents referred to and other
information reaching us from various parts of the northeast report urban laborers and rural workers are subject to
deeply disturbing conditions.

The Church, mother and teacher of all, does not oppose
anyone. Placed in the world for service, it considers itself
obligated toward all: employers and workers, wage earners
and property owners, poor, rich, and those of middle class.
If, driven by our conscience, we condemn injustice, we do

---

[1] It was subsequently accused of being only a rump session [ed.]

not wish to accentuate differences between men or social groups. What we want is forever to unite the people of God.

But the maternal solicitude of the church must turn, in the first instance, toward those who suffer; those who cannot win their family's daily bread despite the abundant sweat of their brows; those who appear condemned to a perpetually subhuman existence.

We loudly summon businessmen and the authorities to employ their energies and means in the creation of new avenues for social advancement. We condemn and cry out against all the injustices committed against the workers, be it with reference to wages, or by the exertion of pressure upon their unions, or in the countless violations of labor statutes and the Land Law.

We urge all workers to continue, despite the present difficulties, to trust their unions and support their associations. Even if these instruments for advancement and defense of the laborer cannot solve all cases satisfactorily, hope for the worker lies in them. Only through the union of all will it be possible to protect the collective interest. At the same time, however, we remind all workers that, defending their rights, they must never forget their duties toward their work but strive to become ever more conscientious and efficient in the execution of their professional tasks.

Finally, we reaffirm our trust in and our support for the Catholic Action organizations that work in the country and among urban laborers. We recognize and proclaim that by pleading for better conditions of life for the workers they are truly evangelizing and preparing the way for the complete revelation of Christ and his doctrine. We exhort you, dear militants, to remain firm and unafraid as an evangelical yeast among the workers, trusting in the words of Christ: "Look up and raise your heads, because your redemption is drawing near" (Luke 21:28).

Recife, July 14, 1966.

IV

Current Issues
in Historical Perspective

◆§22◆

James L. Busey

Brazil's Reputation
for Political Stability

Brazil has a well-established reputation for political stability, especially in comparison with Spanish America. Although some observers—as already demonstrated in other selections—would quarrel with several of the points made in the following article by Professor James L. Busey of the University of Colorado (Colorado Springs), few could disagree with his conclusion that Brazil's reputation for political stability is exaggerated if not completely false. As he points out in this survey, since 1824 Brazil has undergone radical changes in its governmental structure, innumerable unsuccessful revolts, several coups d'état, and frequent military interventions. This historical perspective makes recent events in Brazil less startling and reveals that they are in keeping with Brazilian past experience. Professor Busey is a political scientist who has concentrated his attention on Latin America for several years.

From James L. Busey, "Brazil's Reputation for Political Stability," *The Western Political Quarterly*, XVIII (December 1965), 866–880. This selection is from pp. 866–872 and 874–880. Reprinted by permission of the University of Utah, copyright owners.

In the social science literature on Latin America, Brazil often occupies a rather special place. She is not only Portuguese in cultural origins, and by far the largest republic in Latin America: she is also often reputed to have a special disposition, a unique way of accomplishing political change. It is said that by comparison with her Spanish American neighbors, Brazil is more peaceful, less troubled, less violent and military-minded, more self-critical, more moderate, not so tarnished by brutal tyranny, and more flexible in the face of conflict. Germán Arciniegas tells us that "Brazil is the nation of peace in the world," and he implies that Brazilians may be more peace-loving than people in the United States. According to one authority, ". . . it can be demonstrated from the history of a century and a half that Brazil is less prone to violence than any major country in Latin America."

These or similar observations on Brazil have been made by almost all social and political scientists who have touched on the subject, including this writer. This paper will attempt to re-examine the observations that all of us have made about Brazil, and to orient our thinking in terms of the political reality of the country in the context of the Latin American scene. This task becomes particularly relevant because many scholars not only find Brazil to be eminently peace-loving, but also attribute this to peculiarly tranquil and moderate tendencies that are thought to be buried somewhere in the Brazilian or even the Portuguese temperament, as contrasted with the more belligerent and homicidal tendencies of the Spanish. Finally, recent developments in Brazil compel us to review the question.

It is not easy to establish a set of criteria whose examination will clearly establish to the satisfaction of all that Brazil is more or less peaceful, civilian, moderate, or flexible than her neighbors. The concept of "legitimacy" is a convenient device whereby one may evaluate a set of political phenomena in terms of the kinds of questions that have been raised about Brazil. In a perceptive article on the question of Latin American "stability," Professor Charles W. Anderson sees political legitimacy in the following terms:

> Political legitimacy is that characteristic of a society which enables men to disagree vigorously over the policies that government should pursue or the personnel that should occupy decision-making posts, yet to support common notions of the locus of decision-making authority, the techniques by which decisions are to be made, and the means by which rulers are to be empowered.

The elements of common agreement that are mentioned by Professor Anderson as constituting patterns of legitimacy—i.e., locus of decision-making authority, techniques by which decisions are to be made, and means by which rulers are to be empowered—can be useful in our quest for a definition of Brazilian politics in the Latin American context.

In Brazil, is there general agreement as to the constitutional system for making authoritative decisions? Has there been a substantial concordance with the present system of government? . . . As to the means for the empowerment of rulers, have Brazilians generally agreed upon a pattern, whether democratic or dictatorial, for the settlement of this question? . . . There are Latin Americanists who contend that Brazilians have been able to solve even the most vexing questions of authority without resort to extreme violence, and that this is somehow related to their peaceful nature. The validity of this claim hinges upon evidence of the presence or absence of violence and militarism in Brazilian society, and of the role that force may play in settling Brazil's profoundly fundamental issues. . . . This article will examine these questions in the light of Brazilian reality.

The Constitutional System

Brazil has had five different constitutions, at least three of which have been of considerable importance in establishing systems of government. The Constitution of the Brazilian Empire was decreed on March 25, 1824, and remained in effect for a longer period than any other. The first republican constitution went into effect on February 24, 1891, was subverted in 1930 with the emergence of the Vargas dictatorship, and was officially superseded by the Constitution of July 16, 1934, which was drawn up by a national constitutional assembly. After governing for three years in a quasi-constitutional fashion within the framework of the 1934 document, Getúlio Vargas headed off forthcoming presidential elections by simply decreeing the so-called Constitution of November 10, 1937. Upon the removal of Getúlio from power in 1945, a new constitutional assembly drew up the current Constitution of September 18, 1946.[1]

The fact that Brazil has lived under five different constitutions may not be so significant for our purposes as that these documents have represented radically different kinds of governmental systems. The first was monarchical, under a continuation of the Portuguese House of Braganza, and the Constitution of 1824 was decreed by "Dom Pedro the First, by grace of God and unanimous acclamation of the people, Constitutional Emperor and Perpetual Defender of Brazil." The second, of 1891, not only introduced principles of non-monarchical, republican government, but also established a federal system. The Constitution of 1934 responded to the illegal usurpation of power by Getúlio Vargas in 1930, and was designed to perpetuate his presidency for another term as well as incorporate into the Brazilian constitutional system the various concepts of so-

---

[1] A new constitution was promulgated in 1967 [ed.].

cial reform which the dictatorship had brought to public consciousness. The constitution itself was the work of many men, and was basically a democratic document. However, it legalized another term for Getúlio by providing that the constitutional assembly should select the next president, who of course turned out to be Vargas himself. The Constitution of 1937 was an authoritarian, corporatist document which was decreed by Vargas and established the so-called *Estado Novo*. It provided that the president and congress would be elected as soon as a national plebiscite would approve the constitution. The plebiscite was never held, and during the period 1937–45, Vargas ruled without benefit of either election or congress. The Constitution of 1946 re-established the institutions of the republic more or less as they had prevailed before Vargas.

This brief resumé of Brazilian constitutional history says nothing about the numerous constitutional amendments (and even so-called *leis constitucionais* that were decreed by Vargas), which substantially changed the Brazilian governmental system in terms of federalism, functions of state and municipal governments, the judicial system, and the like. In recent years there was the famous constitutional Amendment No. 4, or *Ato Adicional* of September 2, 1961, which hurriedly adopted a parliamentary system as a device to reduce the powers of incoming President João Goulart; and the no less sensational constitutional Amendment No. 6, of January 23, 1963, which revoked the *Ato Adicional* and restored the presidential system of government.

Finally, on April 9, 1964, in a remarkable statement of constitutional theory, revolutionary forces announced in a so-called *Ato Institucional* that:

> Revolution is to be distinguished from other armed movements by the fact that it translates, not the interest or will of a group, but the interest and will of the Nation. Victorious revolution is invested with the

Constitutional Power. This is manifested by popular election and by revolution. The latter is the most expressive and the most radical form of the Constitutional Power. Thus, the victorious revolution, as the Constitutional Power, is legitimized by its own nature. It removes the former Government and has the capacity to constitute a new Government. In it there is comprised the normative force, inherent in the Constitutional Power. It decrees juridical norms without being limited by normative rules anterior to its history.

Jean Jacques Rousseau would not have been displeased with the tenets of the Brazilian revolution! . . .

Since her independence in 1822, Brazil has obviously undergone some very profound governmental transformations. She has shifted from monarchy to republicanism, has been ruled by dictatorial decree and then restored the forms of democratic government, and has alternated more than once between the parliamentary (1824–89 and 1961–62) and presidential-congressional (1891–1937, 1946–61 and 1963–present) types of governmental systems. To these events, we must add the periods of constitutional confusion which followed the overthrow of Dictator Getúlio Vargas (October 29, 1945), the suicide of elected President Getúlio Vargas (August 24, 1954), the resignation of elected President Jânio Quadros (August 25, 1961), the forced withdrawal of constitutional President João Goulart (April 2, 1964), and the odd hybrid of constitutional form and military decree that has prevailed since then. . . .

Democracy and Dictatorship

Within the limits of this paper, we cannot hope to review the whole history of Brazil relative to changing concepts of democracy and authority. However, the Vargas period and its aftermath are instructive as to Brazilian attitudes on the subject of relationships between government and governed.

The constitutions of 1891, 1934, and 1946 all paid their respects to the idea of constitutional government. Their preambles all proclaim that they are designed to organize democratic regimes, and their provisions call for all the apparatus of elections, representative institutions, individual rights, and rule of law, that are features of western democracies.

In 1930, the ruling party put forward the presidential candidacy of Julio Prestes of São Paulo. In opposition was Getúlio Vargas. In the official count, Prestes was victorious with 1,097,000 votes to only 744,000 for Vargas. However, Vargas claimed fraud, and (though he was from Rio Grande do Sul) was supported by powerful elements of the state of Minas Gerais, who were nettled that a *paulista* instead of a *mineiro* should have been proposed for candidacy. Vargas and his supporters proceeded to overthrow the government, and he established himself as the so-called *chefe do govêrno provisório*. In 1934 he succeeded in getting a constitutional convention to name him as president for the next four-year term. In 1937 he unilaterally proclaimed a new constitution which was never put into effect, and from then on ruled by decree. Speaking of Brazil under Vargas, Luis Alberto Sánchez writes: "The tendency to a corporatist, totalitarian state, with suppression of class struggle, protected by a powerful police apparatus and based on the indefinite extension of the regime, was found in full flower when the second world war broke out." Whether or not the Vargas dictatorship was mild by comparison with others, there can be no question that it was non-legal, arbitrary, and in violation of the constitutional order.

Our task here is not so much to analyze the characteristics of the Vargas period as to comment on the place that

Vargas holds in Brazilian thought and memory. Despite some of the anti-Vargas overtones of the revolution of April 1964, Vargas and the period he symbolized are condoned and even admired and cherished in many respectable quarters of the country. Officially at least, Argentina has rooted out all traces of admiration for Perón. Mexico has long since ceased to adulate Díaz, and Venezuela would not dream of naming avenues or institutions after Gómez or Pérez Jiménez. All her subsequent troubles have not caused the Dominican Republic to restore Trujillo to a place of honor. But much of Brazil, officially and otherwise, still honors the memory of Getúlio Vargas.

Five years after Vargas had been deposed as dictator, and despite his record as subverter of the constitutional order, Brazil voted by a large plurality (3,849,000 to 2,342,000 for the nearest contender) to return Vargas to the presidency. The greatest thoroughfare in downtown Rio de Janeiro is Avenida Presidente Vargas. A distinguished research institute bears his name. The ten-cruzeiro note (admittedly worth about half a cent!) recently carried his likeness. An important railroad-river terminus is named for him. The second largest political party, *Partido Trabalhista Brasileiro,* which held the presidency until April 1964, and has been only partly subdued by events since then, displays busts and pictures of Vargas at party headquarters, intones Vargas' name, and from time to time has broadcasted his melodramatic suicide letter as a prime piece of party propaganda. On April 5, 1963, then President João Goulart proclaimed, "There is the example of a president like Getúlio Vargas, who fell in the campaign for the economic redemption of the country." The next day, General of the Army Osvino Ferreira Alves adulated João Goulart as *"Getúlio redivivo"*—Getúlio reincarnated.

One could comment here about an apparent Brazilian acceptance of the idea of dictatorship. But more important for our purposes, it is clear that there has been no general consensus in Brazil as to the type of regime that is preferred. There is no concurrence about even so fundamental a thing as the respective roles of the governors and the governed. Democracy is extolled, but dictatorship is not rejected. Conflicting political values live side by side with each other. By all the usual political rules, such a society should be anything but peaceful or untroubled. . . .

Militarism and Violence

The part played by the military sector in Brazilian politics may not have been so flagrant as in some Spanish American republics, nor so publicized as in most. There can be no doubt, however, that the use or threat of military force have placed their imprint upon the political development of Brazil. As Professor William S. Stokes puts it:

Brazil, which has been more stable at the national level than almost any other Latin American country in the twentieth century, nevertheless has had a fair share of violence in politics. A study was made of the major internal political conflicts for the period 1822 to 1934. . . . There were 38 major internal political conflicts in the 112 years covered or an average of one each 3.2 years. The *caudilhos* who organized and led the violent efforts came from the landowners, clergy, liberal professions, military, and tradesmen. In recent decades, *machetismo*[2] can especially be studied in the violence of 1922, 1924, 1930, and particularly in the revolt against the federal government which began in São Paulo in 1932. This developed into bloody civil war. *Machetismo* is used persistently in Alagôas, one of the small states. Several politicians were killed in 1956–1957, for example.

---

[2] Settlement of political questions by application of the *machete,* same word in Spanish and Portuguese.

. . . The general population of Brazil had essentially nothing to do with the overthrow of Pedro II in 1889 and the establishment of the Republic. Except for some moral support from leading members of the Republican party, this was almost exclusively a military project. From 1889 to 1914, as the facts make clear, the military played a most important role either in controlling political affairs or in exercising a powerful impact on the course of government. The first republican governments, under Deodoro da Fonseca |1889–91) and Floriano Peixoto |1891–94) were outright military dictatorships. During those first years, there was an unsuccessful naval revolt in 1893, and an uprising in Rio Grande do Sul during 1893–94. Anyone familiar with Euclides da Cunha's work *Os sertões* knows of the violent struggle of some five thousand hinterland *sertanejos* of the northeast, during 1896–97. Federal forces finally suppressed them, and massacred them to the last man.

Though civilian governments prevailed during 1894–1910, they were sharply confined by the demands and expectations of the military arm. Revolts were numerous in various states of the republic, and their violence was in no way mitigated by their lack of success. During 1910–14, the president was Marshal Hermes da Fonseca, whose strong-arm tactics and ineptitude earned him the unenviable reputation of being one of the worst presidents in the history of Brazil. After he left office a Military Club which he dominated intrigued almost continuously to control the course of political affairs. The *Clube Militar* still plays an important role in Brazilian politics, and reports about its activities continue to occupy an important place in Brazilian news.

During 1922 and subsequent years, a violent period of Brazilian politics was introduced by the *tenentes*. These were young officers who advocated progressive, reformist measures in government, and resisted political manipulation by the dominant Republican party. They revolted in Rio de Janeiro in 1922, but were quickly suppressed. In 1924, the São Paulo garrison, under the influence of *tenentismo,* revolted and held the city for three weeks. Meanwhile there were military uprisings in Rio Grande do Sul and in other states. . . .

In October of 1930 the military sector deserted President Wáshington Luis and constitutional government fell to the revolutionary forces of Getúlio Vargas. On October 29, 1945, Dictator Vargas was in his turn deposed under pressure from the military sector. General Eurico Gaspar Dutra . . . was followed by an elected Getúlio Vargas. In August of 1954 it became apparent that Vargas, or at least close associates of Vargas, were involved in an attempted assassination of Carlos Lacerda, at that time an opposition journalist. The military again stepped into the picture and demanded that Vargas resign. His suicide followed, on August 24. Not content with its participation in the ending of the second Vargas administration, the military, led particularly by General Teixeira Lott, had to step in to assure that elected Juscelino Kubitschek would in fact be inaugurated in January of 1956. . . .

During the Kubitschek administration (1956–61), the military sector was favored with notable pay increases and other emoluments, and withdrew from active participation in political affairs. However, with the resignation of Jânio Quadros in August 1961, the military forces again came to the front. They at first refused to permit inauguration of the controversial João Goulart, and then, after a constitutional change was rushed through the Brazilian congress which would adopt the parliamentary system, thus reducing the presidential power, the military sector permitted Goulart's inauguration.

During 1963–64, after resumption of the presidential system, Brazilian tensions reached a fever pitch. Strikes were almost uninterrupted. In August, the military imprisoned a newspaper critic, Hélio Fernándes. In September, about 800 noncommissioned officers revolted in Brasília, and took the Chief Justice hostage, in an attempt at securing a reversal of a Supreme Court decision regarding their ineligibility for election to office. Likewise in September, police detained three individuals in Rio who were found to have forty-four 22-calibre semi-automatic carbines, thought to be part of a right-wing plot to overthrow the government. In the same month, General Pery Bevilacqua of the Second Army gave an order to his troops to resist the subversion of Brazilian institutions—obviously an invitation to them to overthrow the left-leaning Goulart regime. . . .

Finally . . . in a series of lightning moves, during March 30–April 1, 1964, governors of the most important states as well as commanders of three of the four Brazilian army divisions demanded that Goulart leave office. He abandoned the country and, under great military pressure the congress elected General Humberto de Alencar Castelo Branco to serve out the remainder of Goulart's term. Since then, elections have been postponed from October 1965 to December 1966, and the end of President Castelo's term has been extended from January 31, 1966, to March 15, 1967. . . .

Though Brazil has seemed to be outwardly calm, and though she has known long periods of constitutional regularity (1822–89, 1891–1930, 1946–64), most of her republican period has been punctuated by revolts, threats to constitutional order, and incursions of the military into the realms of civilian political authority. What is notable about the several uprisings by military and quasi-military units is not so much that they demonstrate peaceful temperaments as that they were usually unsuccessful. In this sense, the revolts of 1930 and 1964 were exceptional. Had the many other uprisings enjoyed the degree of success that they might normally expect, say, in Ecuador or Bolivia, the Dominican Republic or Guatemala, Brazil would seem to be a most turbulent nation indeed. The many revolutionary failures may be accounted for in part by the huge size of the country. To mount a successful revolution in such a vast territory is beyond the capabilities of most mortals.

Conclusion

We have not demonstrated that Brazil is either more or less peaceful than her neighbors. She has had fewer constitutions than most of her Spanish American cousins, but her changes of political system have been no less profound. Brazil has made no firm commitment to either democracy or dictatorship. . . . Brazil has had her share of violence and of military interposition into civilian affairs.

There are several Spanish American countries which have achieved at least as much internal tranquility as Brazil—for example, Uruguay, Chile, and Costa Rica, and perhaps even Panama and Colombia, if we exclude certain years. In many respects, Argentine political history since 1860 has been rather similar to that of Brazil.

If Brazil has experienced less violence, or at least less success for the method of violence, than have certain Spanish American republics (e.g., Bolivia, Paraguay, Ecuador, Venezuela, Guatemala, Peru, etc.), one should be careful not to poeticize from this about presumed traits of adjustability, compromise, peacefulness, or brotherly love among people of the Portuguese strain. If in Brazil we do not find the chamber of horrors that we do in Bolivia or Paraguay, it may be more proper to attribute this in some measure to the huge size of the country than to some hypothesis about the sophisticated traits of the Portuguese-Brazilians. . . .

As we have seen, military turbulence was common during the Republic, and violence was never far below the surface. Even so, the country managed to carry on through forty years of superficially soporific political existence, during which the oligarchy of medieval landholders, in combination with the army and rising commercial interests, shifted people into and out of the presidency each four years. For shorter or longer periods, during the latter part of the nineteenth and early part of the twentieth centuries, most Spanish American republics experienced similar epochs.

More obvious disorder began to develop when military officers became politically and socially disturbed. Later, these same men helped to bring the Vargas dictatorship to power. Then it was that really basic questions began to shake the Brazilian consciousness. Was democracy or dictatorship to be the final political system? Is it not time for an attack on the ancient feudal fiefs? Are the land-holders to be compensated or simply thrown out? What is to be done about the waves of poverty-stricken people of the countryside, excluded from the use of the Brazilian land, who are descending upon the great cities? Might reforms in the tax system help to alleviate the distress which grows from land monopoly? Can inflation be relied upon as a permanent source of public revenue? If not, how is one to inaugurate a responsible tax system that would bear heavily upon the very conservative elements who must put it into effect? What is to be the role of organized labor? How about demagoguery and extreme nationalism and communism in the framework of the constitutional system? What about foreign investment and influence? Can Brazil liberate herself from these elements without falling into a worse foreign trap? . . .

One cannot but agree with Professor Leslie Lipson when he says that "Constitutional government has not been attained in Brazil." It was almost a half-century ago that James Bryce wrote: "Brazilian society seems to a passing observer to be in a state of transition, and may not for some time to come succeed in reconciling the contrasts between the old and the new, and between theory and practice, which it now displays." He also said: "There are many men of talent, especially oratorical talent, and many men of force, but not enough who shew constructive power and the grasp of mind needed to handle the enormous economic problems which a country so vast, so rich, and so various represents."

Brazil is still in transition, but the transition is moving at an accelerating pace. The events of March and April 1964, and of subsequent months, are but passing portents in a gathering storm. For over half a century Brazil has postponed solutions of her social and economic problems. She has still not reconciled "the contrasts between the old and the new, and between theory and practice," and it is still not certain that her leadership is equal to the task of solving her "enormous economic problems."

Her leadership had better become equal to the task. For Brazil and her problems are now marching to a direct confrontation, and even now one can hear the rumbling of the South American earth. When that confrontation comes, her leaders will have to draw on every bit of genius, conscience, integrity and responsibility they can muster. Otherwise, Brazil will seem to be neither especially tranquil nor particularly untroubled, and Emiliano Zapata and Francisco Villa will be speaking Portuguese.

❧23❧

José Honório Rodrigues

An Independent
Foreign Policy

*Professor José Honório Rodrigues is a distinguished
Brazilian historian who, until approximately ten
years ago, was best known for his work on the
colonial period and on Brazilian historiography.
Feeling, however, that in Brazil's present condition
the historian cannot afford the luxury of remaining
uninvolved in current affairs, he turned his attention
to the uses of the past. In a number of trenchant
books and articles he has sought those qualities in
Brazil's history that would reveal the roots of today's
problems or the guiding principles for tomorrow's
action. In the following essay he applies this method
to diplomacy.*

*During Jânio Quadros' brief administration (1961)
Brazil sought to break away from the pro-American
bloc, to establish itself as a leader among the underdeveloped countries of Africa and Asia as well as*

Translated from José Honório Rodrigues, "Uma política externa
propria e independente," which first appeared in the *Jornal do
Brasil* on June 10 and 17, 1962, and was reprinted in *Política externa independente*, I, No. 1 (May 1965), 15–39. This selection is
from pp. 15–21, 23–32, and 34–39, and is translated and printed
by permission of the author and of the publisher, Editôra Civilização
Brasileira.

Latin America, and to deal freely with the Soviet bloc. Quadros' policy of establishing commercial and diplomatic relations with the socialist countries was bitterly criticized in Brazil as a break with Brazil's tradition and—because it won him support from the left—as the use of diplomacy for domestic political ends. The Brazilian "tradition" is here examined in the light of historical perspective.

The Constant Goals of Brazilian Foreign Policy

The "constants" of Brazilian foreign policy, in either the short or the long run, are permanent goals independent of factions, groups, or interests. There are some national aspirations that are achieved or that disappear in the course of the historical process because of their inadequacy in the face of present goals. But there are other permanent objectives that, if not defended, will lead to national disintegration. The preservation of independence and sovereignty, the maintenance of territorial integrity, and the establishment of peaceful [international] relations are always permanent objectives. True, one or the other of these will often conflict; thus, to defend our independence and sovereignty we had to break off diplomatic relations with Great Britain [in 1863], and our connections with France and the United States were also sometimes endangered. In addition, to defend the territorial status quo and the balance of power in the Río de la Plata we broke the peace and were the aggressors. In deciding on priorities, peace—a permanent objective—had to be violated in order to secure larger goals.

But in the matter of intervention or nonintervention the principle that won out was the latter, established at least since 1841, when Aureliano de Souza e Oliveira Coutinho [1800–1855] held the portfolio [of foreign affairs]. As he said in his report, it was an inalterable principle of imperial policy to observe strict neutrality in the continuous wars that tormented the American states, especially in their internal struggles, a point that was repeated by Honório Hermeto Carneiro Leão [1801–1856] in 1843. Thus, we turned our back on the Portuguese foreign policy, on Carlotismo,[1] and on constant intervention in the Río de la Plata, especially in Uruguay. Interventionism was an unpopular policy as was revealed by the revolution in 1817.

But when, during the regime of [Juan Manuel de] Rosas, there appeared a tendency to reconstruct the old [Spanish] viceroyalty [which had included Uruguay and Paraguay], we set aside this principle, for he not only threatened our territorial integrity but also destroyed the equilibrium in the Río de la Plata. . . . Balance of power and [international] harmony were not, of course, alternative or mutually contradictory ideas. This was proved by the Pact of Alliance with the resulting victory over Rosas [1852] and by the Treaty of the Triple Alliance with the defeat of López [1870].

The fluctuations between . . . intervention and nonintervention end here and so does one historical foreign policy: after 1870 we are [always] against intervention, and I believe there was not a Speech from the Throne, a parliamentary debate, or a party statement that did not defend cordial relations, harmony, and nonintervention. Interventionism, therefore, was a transitory policy, always couched in juridical formalities. Only when these means were exhausted did force appear to impose a decision.

Peace was indispensable for our progress, a progress that has always been blocked by a sterile minority. Peace was also indispensable in our effort to secure "respect, dignity, and national honor" as it was usually put in Speeches from

---

[1] Carlota Joaquina de Bourbon, wife of João VI, claimed during the Napoleonic Wars to be the legitimate heir of Spanish Bourbon rights in America [ed.].

the Throne and reports of the Ministry of Exterior. But peace was especially necessary because we hoped to consolidate our position as a sovereign nation before the European powers. . . .

Our foreign policy was dominated by the European powers and not allied with them. They offered us capital, markets, and, especially after 1850, labor. But there was always an effort on our part to slide out from under. And there was a permanent feeling of struggle against Europe (represented most of all by England and France), which was considered the oppressor and which took away more than it gave. Of course, through Portugal, Europe gave us our forms of life and our political and juridical institutions, but these were really adopted more by the dominant elite than by the people—hogtied and bled white. . . .

An underdeveloped country, a prisoner of the loans made by international banking houses, a country dependent upon the cultivation of agricultural products the prices of which were set in international markets controlled by the great powers, Brazil could not have had an independent and really Brazilian policy. This despite the wish of Pedro II, who was closely identified with the national interest. In his *Diary* he noted on April 1, 1862: "Paranhos [Viscount Rio Branco I (1819–1880)] came by. I spoke to him of the insults that have been offered to Brazil and of the necessity of a policy designed to avoid greater embarrassments in the future." The Empire did have a peculiarly Brazilian policy in the Río de la Plata—only there did the Great Powers allow this. But, in view of the General impossibility of taking an independent stance toward the European powers or toward the United States, the rule was adopted never to sign any treaty with them, the strong powers, in order to avoid greater commitments, which would hinder still further the already hampered defense of the national interest. In fact, our foreign policy was suited only to the interests of the landowning minority. . . .

With [Baron] Rio Branco [II (1845–1912), foreign minister 1902–1912] Brazilian policy turned openly to the United States, with which, he said, we should act in concert. This despite the opposition of Eduardo Prado revealed in a very anti-American book [*A illusão americana*]. The policy of cooperation with the United States, of avoiding petty jabs [from Europe], of creating in Spanish America a spirit of understanding; that is the policy Brazil has been carrying out since then, either by itself or in the Pan American Congresses. This parallelism, this close collaboration with Washington was pushed still further by Lauro Müller [who became foreign minister] in 1912. . . . Müller, an inexperienced greenhorn, tried to convert Rio Branco's dictum into a one-sided policy. A revolt in Paraguay led him to telegraph Domício da Gama [Brazilian ambassador in Washington], asking him to consult the Department of State, for he wished Brazil "to act always in concert."

Domício da Gama cabled in reply: "I do not think we should seek any advice [on] our South American policy nor approval [of] our decisions in order not [to] open [the] way [for] inadmissible pretensions in this and other matters *as is becoming our tendency*." [2] And he continued his lecture—which would not be heeded by Müller or by his successors aside from rare exceptions—saying:

It is quite clear that by resisting the pretensions on the part of a powerful country, pretensions that to us appear excessive, we simultaneously render that country a service by indicating the limits beyond which it would be unwise for it to go precisely because it is powerful. This practical people is not given to unjust resentments and knows how to recognize well-defended rights. But it does not understand the sensitivities of other nations because

---

[2] My italics.

of its lack of experience—for this it learns only from history. Now, so they will not misunderstand our usual courtesy and deference toward friendly nations, I propose that Brazil should give the United States no more signs of politeness than we receive from it; that we return favors but not advance them, for urging these upon them would only lessen our prestige as happens to other countries.

And, after various considerations in defense of a policy of integrity and fearlessness, which would enhance our standing, he suggested Lauro Müller adopt this as a policy directive: "To show ourselves to the world as a 'self-made nation' developing ourselves without prejudice to the rights of others, strengthening friendships in the same dignified manner, conscious of our responsibility and zealous for our sovereignty." [But] from that time on, despite the cautions of Domício da Gama, Washington has been the north star of our foreign policy. . . .

Diplomatic Personnel, Interest Groups, and Ineptitude

The Ministry of Foreign Affairs [during the Empire], in its efforts to secure our rights, consolidate our international position, and deal with European and American pressures, was directed by an impressive majority of lawyers. Of the eighty-five [sic] ministers during the Empire, sixty-five were lawyers, nine were military officers, one was a mathematician, one was a scientist, and one was not a graduate [of any higher school]. Their task should have been more political than juridical; yet partly because the law schools were the storehouse of political leadership and partly because all [our] foreign policy has aways been presented in its juridical form, lawyers have been its directors. Thus, the legal essence became superior to social, political, or economic reality. . . .

The lawyers who dominated the Ministry of Foreign

Affairs arose principally out of Bahian politics. . . . The "elite" from Bahia, living in the most Africanized part of Brazil, strengthened its whiteness by Westernizing itself, by Latinizing itself in the utopia of its imagination. . . . "Europe, France, and Bahia" [rather than "Brazil, Bahia"] is the course of that elite's intellectual derailment, leading it to an almost complete alienation from the nation. Surrounded by an Africanized and illiterate world, it sought compensation in that ministry where one dealt with foreigners in French, obeyed rules of etiquette long discarded in other government offices, and dealt with problems that were juridical and international. . . .

The dominance of lawyers continued; and, if we examine the leadership of the Ministry of Foreign Affairs, we shall see that the republic also emphasized this tendency. . . . From Quintino Bocaiuva [1836–1912], first foreign minister of the republic, . . . to [Francisco Clementino de] San Tiago Dantas [(1911–1964), foreign minister under Quadros], Brazil had sixty-two ministers . . . , of which forty-eight were lawyers, six were officers, four were nongraduates, three were engineers, and one was a physician. . . .

With no further objectives and with an internationally recognized juridical position established, an empty "legalese" now became dominant. The result was political stagnation and vagueness springing from innocuous and sterile conservatism. "All actions have consequences. These are unforeseeable. Therefore, we should do nothing." This became the general principle dominating our foreign office from 1913 to 1956. That same vagueness that characterized the Speeches from the Throne—"our policy is of peace, honor, dignity, and justice"—is maintained by the administrative tradition, that is, by the foreign service personnel. No debate, no [policy] declarations, no realism, but much secrecy and much caution, for "it can't hurt."

So we limited ourselves to debating juridical codes,

juridical questions, international law. Law, law, and more law. The juridical totally overcame the political. . . . International law, although it plays a reduced role in the relations between nations, was exalted. [International] politics was subordinated to law, which is a sort of strait jacket that diplomats use to cover up their political insufficiencies or their economic incapacity in defending the interests of the state. The conservative side of law was a perfect match for some of the bigshots in our foreign ministry. It had once helped preserve some of our national objectives; but now, how to adapt it to the new situation? It became . . . [merely] the right of Brazil to be included in the international scene, as at the Hague Peace Conference. . . .

This "elite" oriented by so much Latinization and so much Westernization is not an innocuous curiosity; it is formed of dangerous madmen. They take themselves seriously. They really believe that they represent the entire mass, and they insist on modeling it in their own image. Living in an Africanized world like Bahia, their attitude always reveals a great lack of real meaning and an intellectual tangentiality. In Minas [de Gerais] the misunderstanding of their representativeness is the same. The "elitist" response is always a missionary one; it has a holy mission: . . . to preach the Gospel of *its* domination and *its* representation to *its* world. Men of Bahia and Minas, Maranhão and Pernambuco—the dominant minority—form the European image of Brazil. They reach the comic point of calling São Luís, the capital of a state [Maranhão] that is 75 percent illiterate, the Brazilian Athens. Or, with their lack of any self-determination, in their mechanical imitativeness, they require the foreign ministry to use office equipment entirely imported from London. . . .

Although foreign policy was not dominated by party politics, and although it did not represent group interests, the fact is that the country has been governed by an

oligarchy, which represented rural interests, expressing its
opinions rather than those of the people (which did not
exist politically until very recently). The exercise of diplomacy was tied to the existence of this milieu and was
almost a monopoly held by a sort of hereditary caste
devoted to foreign affairs. . . . Although these interests
exercised power through representative and constitutional
formulas, the middle classes and the workers lacked group
self-consciousness and could not organize themselves as a
political force to exert influence upon decision making. The
administration of Getúlio Vargas, although it limited decision making to a small circle including the military, nevertheless promoted nationalism and brought the working
classes into the political arena. [But] since 1930 the new
groups and the new tendencies of the middle classes, which
represent Brazilian society, have not been reflected in the
Itamaratí [foreign office]. Economically powerful groups,
like the slave holders and [then] the large-scale coffee mer-
chants, have known how to defend their interests in the
formulation of foreign policy. . . .

The party neutrality of diplomacy was inherited from
the Empire, and I believe no one defined it better than Viscount Rio Branco himself speaking in Parliament a century
ago:

A regularly constituted and civilized country like
ours cannot subject its foreign policy to shifting
internal politics. The parliamentary infighter and
the administrator of internal affairs naturally looks
after his own interests according to his convictions,
which are those of his party; he seeks the triumph
of his friends. The diplomat cannot act on his own
account and does not have as a goal the victory of
these or those personalities. He follows the instructions of his government. Therefore, as long as the
diplomat is educated, able, experienced in affairs,

and loyal, he can serve with any ministry. The political tendencies of the ministry do not prevent him from serving his country well.

What he did not say and what one cannot expect him to have said, was that Conservatives and Liberals were all influenced by pressures of large economic interests, then as now. And if the diplomatic corps was neutral as to party, it was not so socially. The gulf between it and the national reality was and is as large as that of the northeastern political minority, where the average literacy is 23 to 32 percent and where the legitimate regional representation is circumvented by literacy tests for voting. . . .

Now, during the Empire, our diplomacy had to deal with objective questions that affected permanent interests of the nation, whether or not the great majority was legitimately represented. So our diplomacy benefited this majority by defending those interests. [But] the predominance of "juridicism" from 1913 to 1955 represented the triumph of a neoconservatism that insisted on following well-worn paths without any interest in seeking out and exposing those areas of conflict, those pressures that hindered the access of the nation to the road of progress. Uninvolved and remiss, our diplomacy hid behind juridical solutions and, with the greatest submission, served the general interests of the Great Powers, in the belief that what is good for them is good for us. . . .

In international politics generally and in the United Nations especially, Brazil divested itself of interests of its own except in South America, where the old policy of leadership and influence predominated. Both aspects of this line of action—intercontinental submission and continental self-interest—helped the North Americans to deal with the region while making it more difficult for us to defend our world-wide interests.

[*Operation Pan-America*[3]]

With the Juscelino Kubitschek administration, the motivation of our national policy became intensive development. So did that of our international policy. The desire for the full use of our potential in the shortest possible time led to the idea of seeking voluntary international help.

The history of Operation Pan-America has not yet been told, but from the outset it was obvious that it limited our action to the continent, made our policy a regional one, and maintained its traditional American contours. We remained yes–men on the world scene, identified with North American foreign policy, lacking further liberty of action, and running all the risks of its international responsibilities without the flexibility or the autonomy to seek wherever necessary the resources or the commercial relations indispensable to overcoming our difficulties.

Operation Pan-America, as an economic policy for a regional block, removed any intercontinental aspect to the international policy of Latin America. One had the impression that no universal participation was desired or that Latin America was considered an hermetically sealed-off part of the world. It accentuated the regionalism of our international policy, although it transcended through continental solidarity the old colonial residues of border struggles and balance of power in the Río de la Plata.

Internally, to be sure, it presented a positive side in linking domestic needs to international directives, showing that diplomacy could be and should be a national instrument for economic development. But it presented a nega-

---

[3] Operation Pan-America was a plan launched by Juscelino Kubitschek in 1958 after United States Vice-President Richard Nixon was stoned in Caracas. Its aim was to enlist American support for a massive aid program directed at social reform as well as economic development. It is sometimes considered the precursor of the Alliance for Progress [ed.].

tive side in its limitations. For our interior dynamism either will lead the nation to withdraw, to escape from international realities, to search within itself for savings and for an internal market in an almost impossible flight, given the present state of international interdependence, or it will lead the nation to salvation in internationalism, that is, in global voluntary cooperation without distinctions or fears of contamination, since commerce does not have an ideology. Remember that the contact with Anglo-Saxons and even their predominance did not lead us to Protestantism. . . .

An Independent Policy Really Our Own

The essential goal of all Brazilian foreign policy, yesterday as today, has been the right to determine our own directions. . . . The Empire was unable to free itself from all the foreign constraints and pressures that interfered with our international free will. This was sensed by Parliament when it condemned the deference, the forbearance, the weakness of our consular conventions,[4] or the subservience and the humiliating tradition by which strong governments dominated the formulation of our external policies. . . . For all these reasons [Aureliano Cândido] Tavares Bastos [1839–1875] himself, despite his close American interests . . . censured the improper language of the North American minister [during the Civil War, James W.] Webb, adding that "I am not suspect with regard to the United States; if I speak this way I am not led by any affection for the Separatist cause. But I cannot applaud the continuation of this weak policy of genuflection before the leading powers." What was desired then and even more after Baron Rio Branco [took over] . . . was to define as the purpose of our foreign policy the protection of our

---

[4] With England, which allowed a form of extraterritoriality [ed.].

national interests, specifically our interests abroad. . . .
[But] we remained subordinate, without freedom of choice,
in the matter of decisions.

Then came Jânio Quadros, with his attempt to broaden
our foreign policy to include the world. The changing
world scene and the very changes in our key position in
the free world allowed us a freedom of action, which we
could not have had until then. This position led us to a
policy of readjustment, which, [while] it respects hemi-
spheric regionalism, does not play down the importance of
intercontinental goals. It widens commercial opportunities
and political relationships, rejects absolute commitments,
and secures our interests in a representative system and in
the defense of peace. Brazil is a continental country that
must think intercontinentally, not only in its relations with
all America, but also with the world, including the reestablishment of our connection with Africa, which Great
Britain forcefully broke off in the middle of the last century.

Since Quadros, Brazil no longer conforms, no longer
accepts but rather pushes aside the secondary role—a kind
of viceroyalty—to which it is assigned by North American
policy. The United States is convinced that it must isolate
the Western Hemisphere from other countries and maintain
it subordinate to the real metropolis located in Washington.
Such a small and unrealistic role for a country like today's
Brazil—despite all its insufficiencies and the incompre-
hension of economic nationalism—generated a resentment
that the people expressed by voting for Jânio Quadros. He
interpreted this sentiment with some vacillation and doubt,
but, on the whole, with wise intuition. In reality, it is the
line sketched out by Domício da Gama, which is taken up
once again and which is now increased by the idea of
economic development, total freedom of international action, and the multiplication of our political and economic
relationships. . . . President Quadros, conscious of under-

development, which he had seen here and abroad in the Third World,[5] revolted and rose up, initiating a shirt-sleeve policy.

I do not believe, absolutely, that any responsible person will denigrate the value of our alliance with the United States, especially in its economic significance, nor doubt its geopolitical strategic value. Our understanding with the United States, like our harmony with Latin America—today increased by the Free Trade Area—is a legitimate association that we should maintain for our security and development.

But this does not remove the possibility of our disagreeing if our interests are offended or endangered, for we are conscious of our world significance and we demand equality of rights, equality of treatment, and the right to compete, which we see other countries (like Canada, Belgium, and West Germany) possess without argument. . . . The influence that, since then, we have begun to exert and the greater respect with which we are now heard show that the flag hoisted by Quadros, borne also by João Goulart, will not be furled. . . .

The allies of reactionary, antihistoric forces are overcome with hatred toward the mere elaboration and execution of an independent and peculiarly Brazilian policy. . . . They appeal to "tradition," as if there were a simple traditional line or as if tradition denied the present direction, or, yet, as if there has not always been a tension between prudence and [national] irritation, balance and movement, conservatism and radicalism. . . .

The hardest part [of our task] has been to deal with a reluctance [abroad] to accept our liberty of initiative and our right to differ. Also we have had to combat the imposition of a hierarchical order within the "West" to which Brazil must subject itself. That is in the foreign area. But

---

[5] The underdeveloped countries [ed.].

internally, as the people behave better than its leaders and its instinct is sharper than the sophisms of the latter, one can believe that the people's slow but inexorable entrance to the arena of decision–making will impose the idea of progress. And that optimism—a national virtue—will become the philosophy of our historic hope in development. An independent and really Brazilian policy is not dominated by party considerations. It is inspired by radical nationalism, that is, the roots of national independence, by the idea of progress, by the real sources of national behavior, and by the democratic faith that power emanates from the people.

Suggestions for Further Reading

There is a growing literature on Brazil available in English, and no more can be done here than to suggest starting points for the interested reader. Naturally, the person who reads Portuguese will want to use more specialized bibliographies like the one compiled by Rubens Borba de Moraes and William Berrien, *Manual bibliográfico de estudos brasileiros* (Rio, 1949) and the annual volumes of the *Handbook of Latin American Studies* (Washington, 1936–1952; Gainesville, Fla., 1952–   ). In addition there is the extremely valuable essay by Stanley J. Stein, "The Historiography of Brazil, 1808–1889," which appeared in the *Hispanic American Historical Review*, XL (May 1960), 234–278. Especially relevant to the subject matter of the present book is George C. A. Boehrer's "The Brazilian Republican Revolution: Old and New Views," in the *Luso-Brazilian Review*, III (Winter 1966), 43–57. Also useful is E. Bradford Burns' "A Working Bibliography for the Study of Brazilian History," *The Americas*, XXII (July 1965), 54–88. With two exceptions, all the sources mentioned below will therefore be in English. All of them were published in New York unless otherwise specified; sources from which the selections in this book have been taken will not be repeated.

Valuable material on Brazilian history has appeared in other volumes of the Borzoi Books on Latin America. Especially relevant are E. Bradford Burns' *A Documentary History of Brazil* (1966), T. Lynn Smith's *Agrarian Reform in Latin America* (1965), and Frederick Pike's *The Conflict Between Church and State in Latin America*

(1964). In addition, there is the reprinted anthropological study by Charles Wagley, *Amazon Town* (1964). Two books that deal with an earlier period of Brazilian history merit inclusion here because of their value in understanding a later era as well: Gilberto Freyre's *The Masters and the Slaves,* in the abridged edition (1964) and Richard M. Morse's *The Bandeirantes: The Historical Role of the Brazilian Pathfinders* (1965).

The idea of collecting readings or original articles on Brazil within the covers of one book is not new. The best specimen of this genus is *Brazil: Portrait of Half a Continent,* jointly edited by T. Lynn Smith and Alexander Marchant (1951). A less successful earlier effort was Lawrence F. Hill's *Brazil* (Berkeley and Los Angeles, 1947). A recent collection is Irving Louis Horowitz's *Revolution in Brazil* (1964), which includes some first-rate selections within a morass of bombastic commentary. A compilation of articles by American scholars was prepared by Eric N. Baklanoff: *New Perspectives of Brazil* (Nashville, 1966).

A list of general introductions to Brazil should begin with Charles Wagley's *An Introduction to Brazil* (1963), as well as his more trenchant *Brazil: Crisis and Change* (1964). But for those interested in that country's history there is no better starting point than Rollie E. Poppino's *Brazil: the Land and People* (1968). The contrasting European point of view can be found in Jacques Lambert, *Le Brésil: structure sociale et institutions politiques* (Paris, 1953) and in Roger Bastide, *Brésil: terres des contrastes* (Paris, 1957). A rural sociologist who perceptively described what he saw is T. Lynn Smith; see the three editions of his *Brazil: People and Institutions* (Baton Rouge, 1946, 1954, and 1963). Finally, Preston James, a human geographer, brings his technique to bear in *Brazil* (1946) or, better, the more recent chapters on Brazil in his *Latin America* (1959).

The history of Brazil from the time of independence to 1930 was succinctly surveyed with an emphasis on political matters by Percy A. Martin in part of a book edited by A. Curtis Wilgus, *Argentina, Brazil and Chile Since Independence* (reprinted, 1963). A valuable survey, *Empire in Brazil: A New World Experiment With Monarchy* (Cambridge, Mass., 1958), was done by C. H. Haring. Mary Wilhelmine Williams approached the period more sentimentally in *Dom Pedro the Magnanimous, Second Emperor of Brazil* (Chapel Hill, N.C., 1937). Another less than critical study is Anyda Marchant's *Viscount Mauá and the Empire of Brazil: A Biography of Irineu Evangelista de Sousa (1813–1889)* (Berkeley and Los Angeles, 1965). The history of one city can directly contribute to one's understanding of the impelling forces of the entire country. Such is the case with Richard M. Morse's *From Community to Metropolis: A Biography of São Paulo, Brazil* (Gainesville, Fla., 1958). A scholarly landmark was the publication of Stanley J. Stein's *Vassouras: a Brazilian Coffee County, 1850–1900,* Harvard Historical Studies, 49 (Cambridge, Mass., 1957), in which he discussed the economic and social history of one locality. My own study, *Britain and the Onset of Modernization in Brazil, 1850–1914* (Cambridge, Eng., 1968, traces one theme within the larger process of change that characterized this era. José Maria Bello's survey of the *History of Modern Brazil, 1889–1964* has been translated by James L. Taylor (Stanford, Cal., 1966). Although extending well beyond 1930, its best chapters—if one excepts a new concluding one by Rollie E. Poppino—deal with the establishment and early years of the First Republic.

Brazil has been alternately blessed and cursed by a vast number of travelers, many of whom have written excellent accounts of what they saw. One of the best accounts was written by two Protestant missionaries, Daniel Parish Kidder and James Cooley Fletcher. It is titled *Brazil and the Brazilians Portrayed in Historical and Descriptive Sketches* and appeared in successive editions between 1857 (Philadelphia) and 1879 (Boston). Another classic traveler's account is *The Conquest of Brazil* by Roy Nash (1926).

The best study of Brazil's contemporary political history is Thomas E. Skidmore's *Politics in Brazil, 1930–1964* (Oxford, 1967), which deals primarily with events since 1950. John W. F. Dulles has written a rather disappointing study of *Vargas of Brazil, a Political Biography* (Austin, 1967), although it is better than the previously available legalistic approach of Karl Loewenstein, *Brazil Under Vargas* (1942).

On recent economic history one should begin with Werner Baer, *Industrialization and Economic Development in Brazil* (Homewood, Ill., 1965). A longer perspective is provided by the alternately incisive and turgid study by Celso Furtado, *The Economic Growth of Brazil: A Survey From Colonial to Modern Times* (Berkeley and Los Angeles, 1963). It was translated by Ricardo W. de Aguiar and Eric Charles Drysdale. They have also translated the more readable examination of current issues by the same author, *Development and Underdevelopment in Brazil* (Berkeley and Los Angeles, 1964). A detailed study of the textile industry, mainstay of Brazil's industrialization, is Stanley J. Stein's *The Brazilian Cotton Manufacture: Textile Enterprise in an Underdeveloped Area, 1850–1950* (Cambridge, Mass., 1957).

The intellectual life of Brazil, as suggested by some of the readings in the present volume, has been vigorous and complex. Fernando de Azevedo's historical approach, *Brazilian Culture: An Introduction to the Study of Culture in Brazil,* translated by William Rex Crawford (1950), is difficult to wade through but well worth the effort. Another "basic" study is the charming history of Brazilian literature by Samuel Putnam, *Marvelous Journey: A Survey of Four*

Centuries of Brazilian Writing (1948). Especially relevant to the present collection of readings is John Nist's *The Modernist Movement in Brazil* (Austin, 1966). Finally, to deal with still another dimension of Brazilian cultural life there is Henrique E. Mindlin's richly illustrated *Modern Architecture in Brazil* (Rio de Janeiro and Amsterdam, 1956).

Two anthropologists, in addition to Charles Wagley, who have dealt extensively with Brazil are Marvin Harris and Harry William Hutchinson. Among the works of the former is *Town and Country in Brazil* (1956) and of the latter, *Village and Plantation Life in Northeastern Brazil* (Seattle, 1957).

No region of Brazil has attracted more attention from North Americans, especially in recent Communist-fearing years, than its Northeast. Brazilians too have long been intrigued or defeated by it: a literary classic is the war documentary by Euclides da Cunha first published in 1902 and translated by Samuel Putnam as *Rebellion in the Backlands* (Chicago, 1944). The often vain attempts of the Brazilian government to deal with this area's problems are discussed by Albert O. Hirschman in chapter One of his *Journeys Toward Progress* (1965) and by Stefan H. Robock in *Brazil's Developing Northeast: A Study of Regional Planning and Foreign Aid* (Washington, D.C., 1963). The Brazilian point of view is forcefully presented in *Death in the Northeast* by Josué de Castro (1967). Finally, the fact that exploitation in the Northeast is not much greater than in the rest of Brazil is the inescapable conclusion to be drawn from the statistics presented by the Inter-American Committee for Agricultural Development in *Land Tenure Conditions and Socio-Economic Development of the Agricultural Sector: Brazil* (Washington, D.C., 1966).

A Note on the Type

The text of this book was set on the Linotype in a face called TIMES ROMAN, designed by Stanley Morison for The Times (London), and first introduced by that newspaper in 1932.

Among typographers and designers of the twentieth century, Stanley Morison has been a strong forming influence, as typographical advisor to the English Monotype Corporation, as a director of two distinguished English publishing houses, and as a writer of sensibility, erudition, and keen practical sense.

Composed, printed, and bound by
The Colonial Press, Inc., Clinton, Massachusetts

Designed by
Donna Rae Beary Lampell

BORZOI BOOKS ON LATIN AMERICA

Under the general editorship of Lewis Hanke,
UNIVERSITY OF CALIFORNIA, IRVINE

THE CONFLICT BETWEEN CHURCH AND
STATE IN LATIN AMERICA*
Edited by Fredrick B. Pike

THE MASTERS AND THE SLAVES (ABRIDGED)*
A STUDY IN THE DEVELOPMENT OF BRAZILIAN CIVILIZATION
By Gilberto Freyre

DO THE AMERICAS HAVE A COMMON HISTORY? *
A CRITIQUE OF THE BOLTON THEORY
Edited by Lewis Hanke

AMAZON TOWN
A STUDY OF MAN IN THE TROPICS
(*With a New Epilogue by the Author*)
By Charles Wagley

A VOYAGE TO SOUTH AMERICA (ABRIDGED)*
By Jorge Juan *and* Antonio de Ulloa
(*With an Introduction by Irving A. Leonard*)

AGRARIAN REFORM IN LATIN AMERICA
Edited by T. Lynn Smith

THE BANDEIRANTES
THE HISTORICAL ROLE OF THE BRAZILIAN PATHFINDERS
Edited by Richard M. Morse

DICTATORSHIP IN SPANISH AMERICA*
Edited by Hugh M. Hamill, Jr.

THE ORIGINS OF THE LATIN AMERICAN *
REVOLUTIONS, 1808–1826
Edited by R. A. Humphreys *and* John Lynch

THE EXPULSION OF THE JESUITS FROM
LATIN AMERICA
Edited by Magnus Mörner

THE MONROE DOCTRINE *
ITS MODERN SIGNIFICANCE
Edited by Donald Marquand Dozer

**Also available in a hardbound edition*